Stitch by Stitch

Volume 11

TORSTAR BOOKS
NEW YORK · TORONTO

Stitch by Stitch

TORSTAR BOOKS INC.
41 MADISON AVENUE
SUITE 2900
NEW YORK, NY 10010

Knitting and crochet abbreviations

approx = approximately	in = inch(es)	sl st = slip stitch
beg = begin(ning)	inc = increase(e)(ing)	sp = space(s)
ch = chain(s)	K = knit	st(s) = stitch(es)
cm = centimeter(s)	oz = ounce(s)	tbl = through back of
cont = continue(ing)	P = purl	loop(s)
dc = double crochet	patt = pattern	tog = together
dec = decreas(e)(ing)	psso = pass slipped	tr = triple crochet
dtr = double triple	stitch over	WS = wrong side
foll = follow(ing)	rem = remain(ing)	wyib = with yarn in
g = gram(s)	rep = repeat	back
grp = group(s)	RS = right side	wyif = with yarn in front
hdc = half double	sc = single crochet	yd = yard(s)
crochet	sl = slip	yo = yarn over

A guide to the pattern sizes

		10	12	14	16	18	20
Bust	in	32½	34	36	38	40	42
	cm	83	87	92	97	102	107
Waist	in	25	26½	28	30	32	34
	cm	64	67	71	76	81	87
Hips	in	34½	36	38	40	42	44
	cm	88	92	97	102	107	112

Torstar Books also offers a range of acrylic book stands, designed to keep instructional books such as *Stitch by Stitch* open, flat and upright while leaving the hands free for practical work.

For information write to Torstar Books Inc., 41 Madison Avenue, Suite 2900, New York, NY 10010.

Library of Congress Cataloging in Publication Data
Main entry under title:

Stitch by stitch.

Includes index.
1. Needlework. I. Torstar Books (Firm)
TT705.S74 1984   746.4   84-111
ISBN 0-920269-00-1 (set)

9876543

© Marshall Cavendish Limited 1985

Printed in Belgium

ISBN 0–920269–11–7   (Volume 11)

Contents

Step-by-Step Sewing Course

Step-by-Step Needlework Course

Extra Special Crochet

Extra Special Knitting

Extra Special Sewing

Needlework Extra

Homemaker

Shoestring

*Introduction to Irish crochet
*Plain chain lace
*Double picot lace
*Stitch Wise: Two lace patterns
*Pattern for a picot mesh vest

Introduction to Irish crochet

Irish crochet originated in the early part of the 19th century as an attempt to imitate the intricate floral patterns of Venetian point lace. Complicated floral designs were first traced onto glazed linen, then each flower or leaf motif was worked separately (usually over a cord to make a really firm motif) and temporarily basted in place on the linen before being joined together with a chain and picot crochet pattern to create a highly textured and intricately patterned lace fabric.

Today we make a far simpler version. Usually the background lace is made first, then the flower and leaf motifs are sewn onto it. Or a central motif may be worked first, then the background lace pattern is worked in ever-widening circles around it until the fabric is the desired size.

In this course we show you how to work some of the simple background lace fabrics most frequently used when working Irish crochet. They can be used independently to make an item like the lace vest featured in this course, or they can be decorated with individual motifs, instructions for which are given in the next course.

Traditionally, Irish crochet was worked in fine ecru cotton thread using a small steel crochet hook. Although we still use fine crochet cottons to achieve the lovely lacy fabrics associated with this form of crochet, there are now so many beautiful colors available in the various cotton ranges that it is possible to be more adventurous with color. You could also work the patterns in one of the many metallic yarns now available.

Completing a lace fabric

Once the crochet has been completed, dampen the fabric and pin it out to the correct size and shape, making sure that the mesh is not distorted at any point. Leave the lace to dry completely before removing the pins.

To maintain the continuity of the lace patterns and keep the fabric as light as possible, use an invisible seam (see Volume 6, page 15) to join the pieces together as shown here. We have used a contrasting color yarn so that you can see how the seam has been worked, but you should use matching thread when sewing the lace fabrics together.

Or you can join each motif with slip stitch to the motif previously completed while working the last round. For detailed instructions on joining lace motifs this way, see Volume 3, page 20.

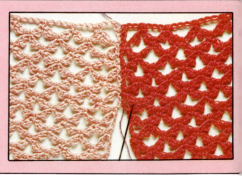

Plain chain lace

This pattern is worked over a number of chains divisible by 4 plus 2. We have worked our sample in a medium-weight crochet cotton so that you will be able to see as clearly as possible exactly how the pattern is worked, but once you have mastered the technique you should work these patterns in a fine crochet cotton for the best results.

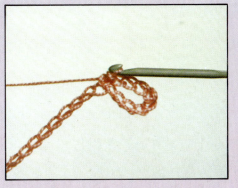

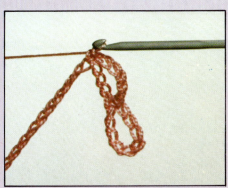

1 Make 30 chains for a sample like the one shown here. Work the foundation chain fairly loosely to prevent the lower edge of the fabric from becoming taut. Now work 1 single crochet into the 10th chain from the hook.

2 Now work 6 chains, skip the next 3 chains, and work a single crochet into the next chain for the 2nd loop in the row. Work under 2 loops in the foundation chain for a neat edge.

3 Repeat step 2 all the way across the row, so that you work the last single crochet into the last chain. There should be 6 chain loops in all.

4 The fabric is made by repeating the last row each time. Start every row with 9 chains and work a single crochet into each loop, followed by a 6 chain loop each time. End each row by working the last single crochet into the last loop.

5 Here is a sample of the same pattern, worked in a fine crochet cotton for a light lacy fabric.

Double picot lace

Here we show you how to work one of the most popular Irish crochet background patterns. The technique is very similar to the simple chain lace mesh already shown, except that 2 picot points are worked into every loop to form the pattern. Once again the sample has been worked in medium-weight crochet cotton for clarity, but the best results are obtained by working a fine crochet cotton. The pattern is worked over a number of chains divisible by 4 plus 3.

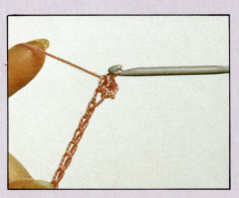

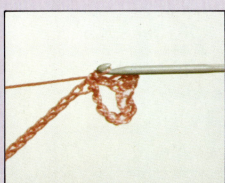

1 Make 31 chains for a sample like the one shown here and work a single crochet into the 3rd chain from the hook for the first picot. Make sure that you work the foundation chain fairly loosely to prevent the lower edge from becoming taut.

2 Now work 1 chain followed by a single crochet into the 8th chain from the first picot made at the beginning of the row.

continued

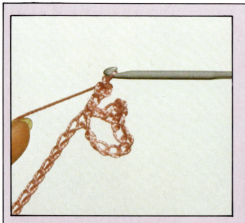

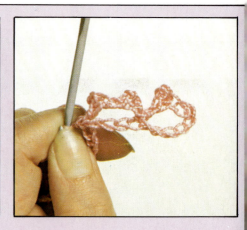

3 Work the next picot by making 3 chains and then working a single crochet into the first of these 3 chains.

4 Now work 4 chains followed by a single crochet into the 3rd chain from the hook for the 2nd picot.

5 Make 1 chain. Skip the next 3 chains and then work a single crochet into the next chain. Steps 3 to 5 complete the first picot loop.

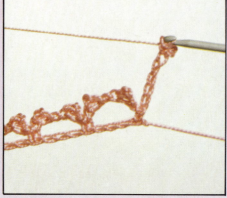

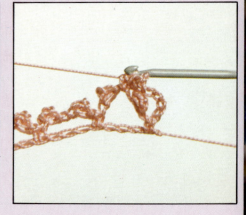

6 Repeat steps 3 to 5 all the way along the foundation chain, working the last single crochet into the last chain. You should not work a picot point at the end of the row; otherwise the fabric edges will not remain straight.

7 Start the next row with 7 chains and then work a single crochet into the 3rd chain from the hook for the first picot as before.

8 Now work 1 single crochet between the picots of the first loop worked in the previous row.

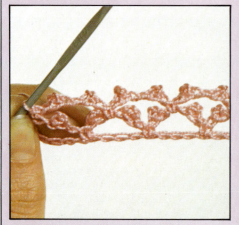

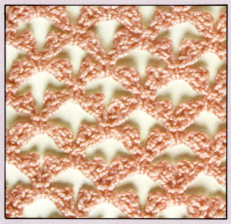

9 Now repeat steps 3 to 5 all the way across the row, working each single crochet between the picot points worked in the previous row each time. Work the last single crochet into the last loop after the last picot worked in the previous row.

10 To continue the pattern repeat the last row each time until the fabric is the required size.

11 Here is the same pattern worked in a fine crochet cotton to obtain a lacy effect. Try working the same pattern in a metallic yarn.

Stitch Wise

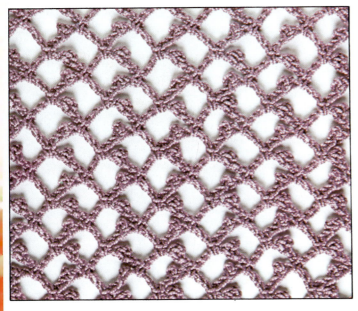

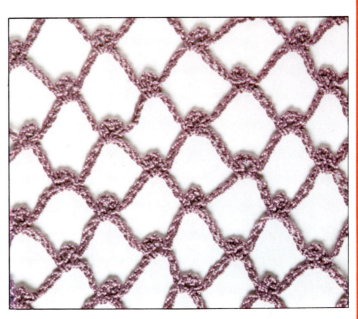

Single picot lace

This pattern is a variation on the double picot lace worked in the step-by-step instructions and can also be used as a lace fabric for Irish crochet.
The pattern is worked over a number of chains divisible by 5 plus 1.
1st row 1sc into 3rd ch from hook (picot), 2ch, 1sc into 8th ch from picot, *6ch, 1sc into 3rd ch from hook (picot), 2ch, skip next 4ch, 1sc into next ch, rep from * to end, working last sc into last ch. Turn.
2nd row 8ch, 1sc into 3rd ch from hook (picot), 2ch, 1sc into first loop after picot worked in previous row, *6ch, 1sc into 3rd ch from hook (picot), 2ch, 1sc into next loop after picot worked in previous row, rep from * to end, working last sc into last loop after last picot worked in previous row. Turn.
The 2nd row forms the pattern and is repeated throughout.

Loop lace

This simple lace pattern is worked over a number of chains divisible by 7 plus 1.
1st row 1sc into 15th ch from hook, 4ch, 1sc into same place as first sc, *10ch, skip next 6ch, (1sc, 4ch and 1sc) all into next ch, rep from * to end. Turn.
2nd row Sl st to center of first 4ch loop, 13ch, *work (1sc, 4ch and 1sc) all into next 10ch loop, 10ch, rep from * to end, working (1sc, 4ch and 1sc) all into last loop. Turn.
The 2nd row forms the pattern and is repeated throughout.

Picot mesh vest

A simple, beautiful vest. The back and fronts are made in one piece so there are no unattractive side seams, and the delicate effect is enchanced by the picot edging. In course 49 on page 21 there are instructions for Irish crochet motifs to sew onto the vest.

Sizes
To fit 32[34:36]in (83[87:92]cm) bust. Length, 20[20:21]in (51[51:53]cm).
Note Directions for larger sizes are in brackets []; if there is only one set of figures it applies to all sizes.

Materials
9[9:11]oz (250[250:300]g) of a fine pearl cotton
No. 0 (2.00mm) steel crochet hook
4 buttons

Gauge
5 loops to 4in (10cm) worked on No. 0 (2.00mm) hook.

Back and fronts (worked in one piece to armholes).
Using No. 0 (2.00mm) hook make 181[193:205]ch for entire lower edge.
Base row 1sc into 3rd ch from hook, 1ch, skip next 5 ch, 1sc in next sc, *3ch, 1sc into 3rd ch from hook—picot formed—, 4ch, 1sc into 3rd ch from hook, 1ch, skip next 3 ch, 1sc into next ch—picot loop formed—, rep from * to end. Turn. 43[46:49] picot loops formed.
Patt row 7ch, 1sc into 3rd ch from hook, 1sc between picots of first loop, *1 picot loop, 1sc between picots of next loop, rep from * to end, working last sc into loop after last picot. Turn.

This row forms the patt. Cont in patt until work measures 8¼[8¼:8¾]in (21[21:22]cm) from beg.
Shape front edges
Next row Patt to within last loop, 3ch, 1sc into 3rd ch from hook, 1dc into loop after last picot, turn.
Next row 7ch, 1sc into 3rd ch from hook, skip first loop, 1sc between picots of next loop (1 picot loop decreased), patt to within last loop, 3ch, 1sc into 3rd ch from hook, 1dc into loop after last picot. Turn. 41[44:47] picot loops.
Patt 8 rows, then work the 2 decrease rows once more, 39½[42½:45½] picot loops.
Divide for armholes
Next row 7ch, 1sc into 3rd ch from hook, 1sc between picots of next loop, work 7[8:9] picot loops, 3ch, 1sc into 3rd ch from hook, 1dc into next picot loop, turn and work on these sts for first front.

Next row 7ch, 1sc into 3rd ch from hook, 1sc into next picot loop, patt to end. Turn. 7½[8½:9½] picot loops.
***Next row** 7ch, 1sc into 3rd ch from hook, 1sc into next loop, work 6[7:8] picot loops, 3ch 1sc into 3rd ch from hook, 1dc into next loop, turn.
Next row 7ch, 1sc into 3rd ch from hook, 1sc into next loop, patt to end. Turn. Rep last 2 rows 1[2:3] times more, working 1 picot loop less each time until there are 5½ loops. Work 1 row without shaping.
Now keeping armhole edge straight cont to dec at front edge as before on next and foll 10th row. 3½ loops. Cont straight until work measures 20[20:21]in (51[51:53]cm) from beg. Fasten off.
Rejoin yarn for second front as follows: skip loop of turning dc at armhole, skip next 22[23:24] picot loops, join yarn to next picot loop, work 8[9:10] picot loops. Turn.
Now work as for first front from *** to end.
Rejoin yarn to base of turning dc at start of armhole, 7ch, 1sc into 3rd ch from hook, 1sc into next picot loop, work 22[23:24] picot loops, turn and cont on these sts for back. Dec 1 picot loop at each end of every row until 14½[15½:16½] picot loops rem. Cont straight until back measures same as front.

Join shoulders

Next row 3ch, sl st into first loop of front shoulder, *2ch, 1sc into next picot loop on back, 2ch, sl st into next picot loop on front*, rep from * to * twice more, 2ch, 1sc into next picot loop on back, work 7[8:9] picot loops across back neck, 2ch, 1sc into first loop on shoulder of second front, work from * to * 3 times, 3ch, 1sc into last loop on back.
Fasten off.

Armhole edgings (alike)
Join yarn to base of armhole and work *3ch, 1sc into 3rd ch from hook, 1ch 1sc into next loop, rep from * all around armhole.
Fasten off.

Front and lower edging
Join yarn to lower front edge and work along lower edge thus: 1sc into first loop, *(3dc, 1 picot and 3dc) all into next sc, 1sc into next loop, rep from * along lower edge, 3sc into corner, **3ch, 1sc into 3rd ch from hook, 1sc into next loop **, rep from ** to ** 8 times, work 1 picot loop, skip next row end, 1sc into next loop—1 buttonhole made—, rep from ** to ** 6 times, work 3 more buttonholes working 6 picots between each one, then cont along front edge to shoulder, now work picot loops across back neck, then work edging along front edge, 3sc into corner, sl st into first sc.
Fasten off.

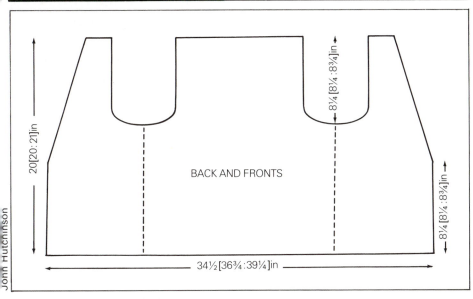

20[20:21]in

8¼[8¼:8¾]in

8¼[8¼:8¾]in

BACK AND FRONTS

34½[36¾:39¼]in

Baby's bib

Make this colorful appliquéd bib for meal times.

Size
12 × 10in (30 × 25cm).

Materials
Piece of terrycloth 12 × 10in (30 × 25cm)
2¼yd (2m) of 1in (2.5cm)-wide contrasting bias binding
Scraps of cotton fabrics in four solid colors
Matching sewing thread

1 Fold the piece of terrycloth in half lengthwise. Round off both double corners in a gentle curve.

2 To form the neckline, mark a point 2½in (6cm) down from top edge at fold. Mark a point 2in (5cm) along top edge from fold. Mark a gentle curve between the two points. Cut out along marked line. Unfold terrycloth.

3 Fold bias binding in half over the outer edge of the bib, starting and ending at the shoulder edges of the neck. Fold binding in half evenly, wrong sides inside. Pin, baste and stitch.

4 Bind the neck edge in the same way, leaving 10in (25cm) of bias binding free at each side for neck ties.

5 Turn in each short end of ties and then fold each tie in half lengthwise, long edges matching. Pin, baste and stitch down each tie.

6 For engine, cut a piece of red fabric 2½ × 1½in (6 × 4cm), a 1¼in (3cm) square of green fabric for cab and a ⅝in (1.5cm) square of blue fabric for smokestack.

7 For cars cut out a piece of fabric 1¾ × 1¼in (4.5 × 3cm) from both blue and green fabrics.

8 For the wheels cut out five ¾in (2cm)-diameter circles and one 1¼in (3cm)-diameter circle from the dark blue fabric.

9 Arrange the train on the bib, with the cab and smokestack overlapping the engine. Center the train between the side edges 2¼in (5.5cm) up from bound edge with the cars about 1½in (1.2cm) apart.

10 Place the wheels so that they overlap the lower edges of the engine and cars. Position the large wheel at the back of the engine.

11 Pin, baste and stitch the complete train in place, using a close zig-zag stitch.

12 Zig-zag stitch between the engine and the first car and between the first and second car, ¼in (5mm) from lower edges for the couplings.

Kim Sayer

Crochet / COURSE 48

*Colored patterns
*Three-color check
 pattern
*Stitch Wise: More colored
 patterns
*Pattern for a man's shawl-
 collared sweater

Colored patterns

There are several different patterns which can be worked in crochet using two or three different colors to create fabrics with checked or multi-colored patterns. The patterns can be worked very simply in single crochet, half doubles or doubles, using blocks of stitches worked in alternate colors to create the patterns. Or you can use more complicated crochet patterns, such as a shell pattern, worked in two or three colors to create an unusual checked effect.

Some patterns can be created by working in different colors over stitches already worked in previous rows. In this case only one color will be used on each row. This means that the spare yarn can be carried up the side of the work, or it can be broken off and re-joined to the fabric at the beginning of the next row in which it is needed again.

When blocks of different colors are used to create the pattern, the colors not in use should be either carried or woven across the back of the fabric. The method used will depend on the size of the pattern repeat (see Volume 2, page 16 for detailed instructions).

When working from a pattern where more than one color has been used, you will see that each color is coded with a letter — A, B, C, etc. Your directions should tell you which letter refers to which color. If you do not intend to use the same colors as those used for the pattern garment, code your chosen colors in a similar way, using either letters or numbers, to avoid confusion while working from the pattern directions.

We have worked our samples in a knitting worsted using a size G (4.50mm) hook. You could, of course, use any ply for the patterns, but remember that when the spare yarn is carried across the back of the work, the fabric will be much thicker than usual. This should be taken into account when choosing a yarn and pattern.

Three-color check pattern

Here we show you how to work an unusual check pattern created by working into stitches in the row below. Spaces rather like those worked in filet crochet form the basic pattern on every row, but by using a different color on each row and working into these spaces on the following row you can create a simple checked effect. The best results will be achieved when the pattern is worked in a knitting worsted, which will make a really firm fabric.

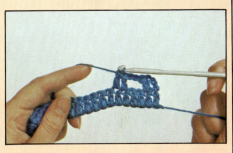

1 Make 32 chains. Add 4 extra chains for each additional pattern repeat if you want to increase the width of the fabric. Now work a double row (30 doubles) in the first color (A). Begin 2nd row with 3 chains. Skip the first double and work 1 double into the next double.

2 Now make 2 chains. Skip the next 2 doubles and work 1 double into each of the next 2 doubles.

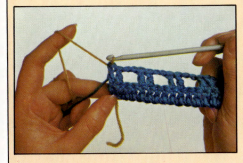

3 Continue to repeat step 2 to the end of the row, working the last double into the top of the turning chain and introducing the 2nd color (B) while working the last stitch.

4 Now turn and leave A at the side of the work. Carry it up the side until it is needed again. Make 2 chains.

5 Skip the first 2 doubles and then work a double into each of the next 2 stitches skipped on the first row, placing the hook in front of the 2-chain horizontal bar so that the stitch is worked over it. *continued*

Frederick Mancini

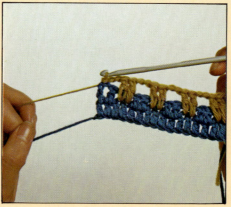

6 Continue to work 2 chains over the 2 doubles and a double into each of the skipped stitches in the previous row, to the end of the row, working in front of the 2-chain bar each time.

7 Complete the row with 2 chains, working a slip stitch into the top of the turning chain at the end of the row.

8 Introduce the 3rd color (C) at this point by drawing a loop of yarn through the slip stitch. Turn and leave B at this side. Carry it up the side until it is needed again.

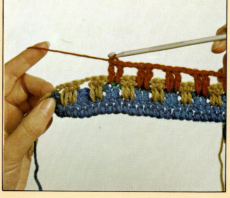

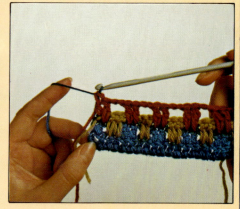

9 Make 3 chains to count as the first double. Now work a double into the 2nd stitch in the **first** pattern row, in front of the 2-chain bar made in the previous row.

10 Continue working 2 chains over the 2 doubles and 2 doubles into each of the 2 skipped stitches worked in the previous row as before to the end of the row.

11 Complete the row by working a double into the last stitch and a double into the turning chain skipped in first pattern row. Re-join A while working the last stitch.

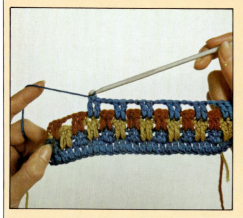

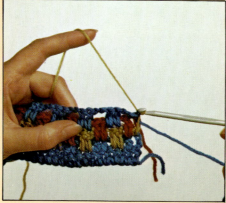

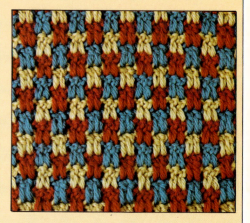

12 Leave C at the side of the work as before. Begin the next row with 2 chains. Skip the first 2 doubles and then continue to work this row as before, working a double into each of the skipped stitches worked in the previous row, working in front of the 2 chain-bar as before and working 2 chains over the 2 doubles worked in the previous row.

13 Complete the row by working 2 chains followed by a slip stitch into the top of the turning chain. Draw B through the slip stitch as before so that it is ready to be used again. Turn the work.

14 To continue working the pattern, alternate the two rows each time so that you begin one row with 2 chains and the following row with 3 chains and a double, changing color on every row. By using three colors you will find that the yarn is always on the correct side of the work when it is needed again.

Stitch Wise

Three-colored shell pattern

This pattern is worked over a number of chains divisible by 6 plus 1 with 3 extra turning chains.
The colors have been coded A, B and C.

1st row (RS) Using A work 2dc into 4th ch from hook, *skip 2ch, 1sc into next ch, skip 2ch, 5dc into next ch—called shell—, rep from *, ending with 3dc worked into last ch—half shell—, and changing to B on last st. Turn.
2nd row Using B, 1ch to count as first sc, *1 shell into next sc, 1sc into 3rd dc of next shell, rep from * to end working last sc into 3rd of first 3ch and changing to C while working last st.
3rd row Using C, 3ch to count as first dc, 2dc between sc and next shell at beg of row, *1sc into 3rd dc of next shell, 1 shell into next sc, rep from * to end working half shell into top of turning ch, and changing to A on last st. Turn.
The 2nd and 3rd rows form the pattern repeat. Work 1 row in each color.

Checked ribbing

In this pattern an unusual effect is achieved by combining 2×1 ribbing with 2 colors, changing the colors after every second row of the pattern. The two colors have been coded A and B. Make an even number of chains.

1st row Using A, work 1sc into 3rd ch from hook, 1sc into each ch to end. Turn.
2nd row As 1st.
3rd row Using B, 1ch, skip first st, 1sc into next st, work 1dc around stem of next st, inserting hook from right to left behind stem of stitch—called 1dc B—, *1sc into each of next 2 sts, 1dc B around stem of next st, rep from * to end, working last sc into turning chain. Turn.
4th row Using B, 1ch to count as first st, skip first st, 1sc into each st to end, working last sc into turning chain. Turn.
5th row Using A, *1ch, skip first sc, 1sc into next sc, 1dc B around stem of dc worked in 2nd row, 1sc into each of next 2 sts, rep from * to end, working last dc B around stem of dc B worked around turning chain in 2nd row. Turn.
6th row Using A, as 4th row.
The 3rd to 6th rows form the pattern and are repeated throughout, working 2 rows in each color.

Two-colored brick stitch

This pattern is worked over a multiple of 4 plus 2 chains. Our sample has been worked in doubles but you could also work the same pattern in single crochet, half doubles or triples depending on the size of pattern required. The two colors are coded A and B.

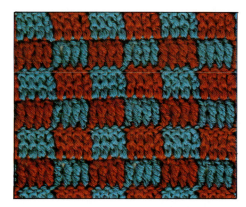

1st row Using A, work 1dc into 4th ch from hook, 1 dc into each of next 2ch changing to B on last st, *using B work 1dc into each of next 4dc changing to A on last st, using A work 1dc into each of next 4ch, rep from * to end. Turn.
2nd row Using B, work 3ch to count as first dc, skip first st, work 1dc into each of next 3 sts changing to A on last st, *using A work 1dc into each of next 4dc, changing to B on last st, using B work 1dc into each of next 4 sts, rep from * to end. Turn.
Rep the 1st and 2nd rows throughout so that the position of the colors is alternated on each row.

Three-colored lark's foot stitch

This pattern is worked over a multiple of 4 chains plus 3.
The colors are coded A, B and C.

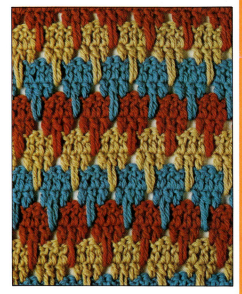

Frederick Mancini

1st row Using A, work 1dc into 4th ch from hook, 1dc into next ch, *skip 1ch, 1ch, 1dc into each of next 3ch, rep from * to end. Turn.
2nd row Using A, work 3ch to count as first dc, skip first dc, 1dc into each of next 2dc, *1ch, 1dc into each of next 3dc, rep from * to end, working last dc into top of turning chain and changing to B on last st. Turn.
3rd row Using B, 4ch to count as first dc and 1 ch sp, skip first 2 dc,* 1dc into next dc, work 1dc into 1 ch sp on first row inserting hook under 1 ch bar and drawing up yarn to same height as last st—called 1 long dc—, 1dc into next dc, 1ch, skip next dc, rep from * to end, 1dc into turning chain. Turn.
4th row Using B, 4ch to count as first dc and 1ch sp, *1dc into each of next 3dc, 1ch, rep from * to end, 1dc into 3rd of first 4ch and changing to C on last st. Turn.
5th row Using C, 3ch to count as first dc, 1 long dc into first 1 ch sp, *1dc into next dc, 1ch, skip 1dc, 1dc into next dc, 1 long dc into next 1ch sp, rep from * to end, 1dc into 3rd of first 4ch. Turn.
6th row Using C, 3ch to count as first dc, skip first dc, 1dc into each of next 2dc, *1ch, skip 1dc, 1dc into each of next 3dc, rep from * to end, working last dc into top of turning chain and changing to A on last st. Turn.
3rd to 6th rows form pattern and are repeated throughout, changing color after every two rows. Note that the long double is worked under the chain bar of the previous row each time.

Man's shawl-collared sweater

Here is a comfortable sweater to crochet. It is interesting to make because of the rich combination of stitches which give it a rugged texture.

Sizes
Chest, 38[40:42]in (97[102:107]cm).
Length, 33½in (83cm).
Sleeve seam, 22½in (56cm).
Note Directions for larger sizes are in brackets []; if there is only one set of figures it applies to all sizes.

Materials
  Knitting worsted
    20[22:25]oz (550[600:700]g) in main color (A)
    9[9:11]oz (250[250:300]g) in 1st contrasting color (B)
    4oz (100g) in 2nd contrasting color (C)
  Sizes E and G (3.50 and 4.50mm) crochet hooks

Gauge
16dc and 12 rows to 4in (10cm) in check patt and seed st on size G (4.50mm) hook.

Back
****Using size G (4.50mm) hook and B, make 87[91:95]ch.
Base row Sl st into 3rd ch from hook, *1dc into next ch, sl st into next ch, rep from * to end. Turn. 86[90:94] sts.
Beg seed st patt.
Patt row 2ch, skip first sl st, sl st into next st, *1hdc into next st, sl st into next st, rep from * to end. Turn.
Rep patt row once more. Beg check patt.
1st row 3ch to count as first dc, 1dc into 2nd st, *2ch, skip next 2 sts, 1dc into each of next 2 sts, rep from * to end, joining in C on last st. Turn.
2nd row Using C, *2ch, skip first 2dc, 1dc into each of next 2 sts skipped 2 rows below, rep from * to end, finishing 2ch, skip next dc, sl st into top of the 3 ch, joining in A on last st. Turn.
3rd row Using A, 3ch, 1dc into next dc 2 rows below, *2ch, skip next 2dc on previous row, 1dc into each of next 2 dc 2 rows below, rep from * to end, joining in B on last st. Turn.
4th row Using B, *2ch, skip first 2dc, 1dc into each of next 2dc 2 rows below, rep from * to end, finishing 2ch, skip next dc, sl st into top of the 3ch, joining in C on last st. Turn.
5th row As 3rd row but use C instead of A and join in A on last st.
The 3rd to 5th rows form the color sequence. Cont in patt until the 4th row

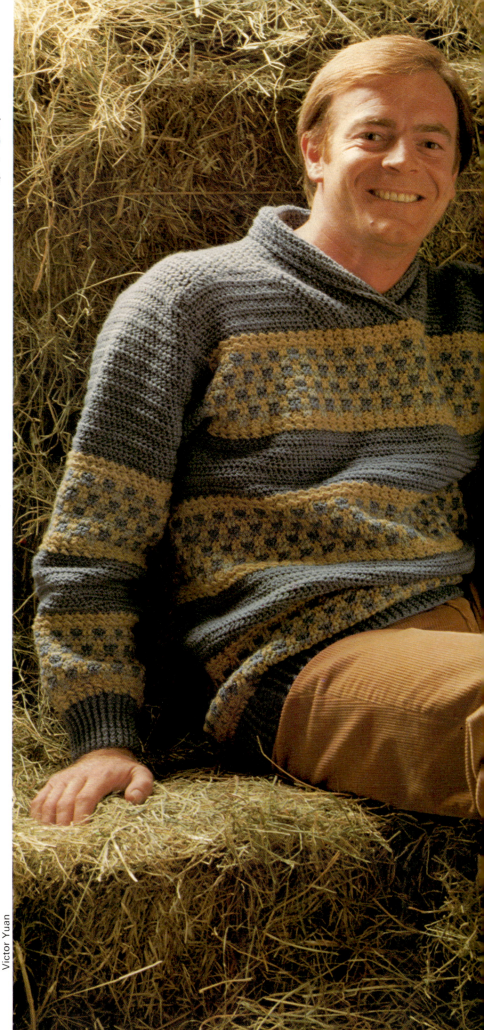

Victor Yuan

in A has been worked. Cut off C.
Next row Using B, 3ch, 1dc into next dc 2 rows below, *1sc into each of next 2 sts, 1 dc into each of next 2dc 2 rows below, rep from * to end. Turn.
This completes check patt. Using B, work 3 rows seed st patt, joining in A on last st of last row. Cut off B. Beg hdc patt.
Patt row 2ch to count as first hdc, 1hdc into each st to end. Turn.
Rep last row 10 times more.
This completes hdc patt. Now work 3 rows seed st patt, 13 rows check patt, 3 rows seed st patt and 11 rows hdc patt. Fasten off.
Shape armholes
Next row With RS facing join B to 9th st from side edge and work in seed st to within last 8 sts. Turn.
Now work 2 rows seed st patt, 13 rows check patt and 3 rows seed st patt.**
Work 8 rows hdc patt. Fasten off.
Shape saddle shoulders
Next row Rejoin A to 11th [12th:13th] hdc from armhole edge, work to within last 10[11:12] hdc. Fasten off.
Rep last row once more, do not fasten off but work 3 rows hdc patt. Fasten off.

Front
Work as for back from ** to **.

Divide for neck
Next row Patt 24[26:28]hdc. Turn.

Next row Dec 1hdc (by working 2hdc tog), patt to end. Turn.
Next row Patt to end. Turn.
Rep last 2 rows twice more, then work the first of these 2 rows again. Fasten off.

Shape saddle shoulder
Next row Rejoin A to 11th[12th:13th] hdc from armhole edge, patt to end. Fasten off.
With RS facing skip center 22 hdc, join yarn to next hdc and patt to end of row. Turn. Complete to match first side of neck reversing shaping.

Sleeves
Using size G (4.50mm) hook and B, make 55ch. ***Work 3 rows seed st patt, 13 rows check patt and 3 rows seed st patt. Now work 11 rows hdc patt, inc 1 hdc at each end of 1st and every other row (by working 2 sts into first and last st).***
Rep from *** to *** once more. 79 sts.
Mark each end of last row to denote top of sleeve.
Cont in hdc with A only, work 5 rows without shaping. Fasten off.

Shape top
Next row Rejoin A to 10th hdc and patt to within last 9hdc. Fasten off.
Rep last row twice more, do not fasten off on last row but turn and work 5 rows, dec 1hdc at each end of every row. 15 sts. Work 12 rows without shaping for saddle shoulder extension. Fasten off.

Waistbands (alike)
With RS facing join A to first st on base row and using size E (3.50mm) hook work 83[87:91]sc along lower edge.
1st ribbing row 2ch, *1sc around front, 1sc around back, rep from * to end. Turn.
2nd ribbing row 2ch, *1sc around back, 1sc around front, rep from * to end. Turn.
Rep 2 ribbing rows 5 times more. Fasten off.

Cuffs (alike)
With RS facing join A to first st on base row and using size E (3.50mm) hook work 55sc along lower edge. Now work 2 ribbing rows of waistbands 6 times. Fasten off.

Shawl collar
Set in sleeves, sewing straight side edges above markers to 8 sts at armhole and saddle shoulder extensions to top of back and front. With RS facing join A to right front neck at base of opening and using size G (4.50mm) hook work 86 hdc around neck to base of opening on left front neck. Turn. Work 14 rows hdc patt. Fasten off.

To finish
Join side and sleeve seams. Sew row ends of collar to base of opening, overlapping right and left.

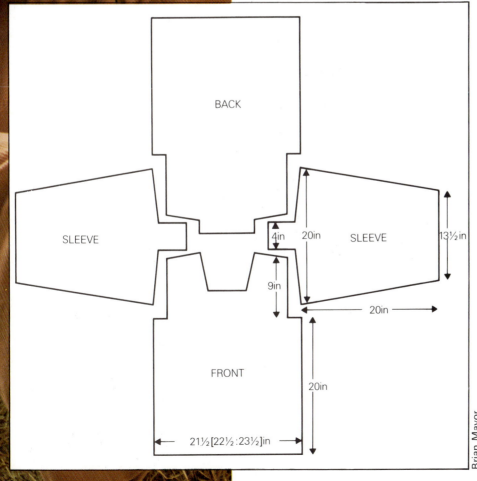

BACK

SLEEVE

SLEEVE

4in

20in

13½in

9in

20in

FRONT

20in

21½[22½:23½]in

Brian Mayor

Crochet / COURSE 49

* Irish crochet motifs
* Single leaf
* Shamrock
* Working over a cord
* Stitch Wise: more motifs
* Patterns for motifs for lace vest

Irish crochet motifs

This course features some of the traditional flower and leaf motifs used to create the intricately textured and ornate lace fabrics which distinguish Irish crochet from the other forms of crochet lace.

The rosebud, single leaf and shamrock on the vest on page 20 are just some of the many flowers and leaves used to form the familiar floral patterns used in Irish crochet.

Traditionally each motif or sprig was worked first and the lace completed by joining each motif with a lace background or filling (see page 4). Although the lace can still be worked this way, it is more usual to work the background pattern first, followed by the motifs which can then be sewn onto the lace at any point with tiny, hidden stitches.

Some motifs, such as the rosebud featured on the vest, are worked in rounds, and others, like the leaves, are worked in rows. The rosebud on page 21 is worked in much the same way as the rose featured in the bedspread in Volume 6, page 30, in which several layers of petals are worked over chain loops made at the back of the flower. Full instructions for working the rosebud are given on page 21. If you have any difficulty in working the motif, refer to the instructions in Volume 6, page 27.

Single leaf

This pretty leaf is worked in rows, working into the back of each stitch to form the ringed effect. It can be used individually or in groups on your fabric, depending on how complicated you want your lace to be.

We have worked these samples in a thick crochet cotton so that you will be able to see exactly how the motif should be worked, but once you have mastered the basic technique, work the leaf in a fine crochet cotton for the best results.

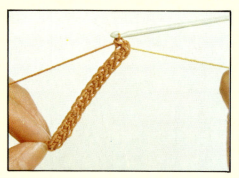

1 Make 16 chains. Work 1 single crochet into 3rd chain from hook, then 1 single crochet into each chain until only one remains unworked, working under 1 loop only in the foundation chain. Now work 3 single crochets, into the last chain to form the tip of the leaf.

2 Do not turn the work, but continue to work a single crochet into each chain along the other side of the foundation chain, working under 1 loop once more so that you form a lattice effect at the center. (Base of leaf.)

3 Work another single crochet into the same place as the last stitch to form the base of the leaf. Do not turn. Continue to work along the first side, working into the back loop only of each stitch until you have worked 11 single crochets in all on this side.

4 Work into the back loop of each stitch from now on. Turn and make 1 chain. Skip the first stitch then work back along the 11 single crochets until the base of the leaf has been reached.

5 Now work 1 single crochet, 1 chain and 1 single crochet all into the single crochet at the base of the leaf.

6 Continue to work 1 single crochet into each stitch along the other side of the leaf until 4 stitches remain unworked, counting from the center stitch of the 3 single crochet group worked at tip of leaf.

7 Now turn so that these 4 stitches are left unworked and the tips on each side of the leaf are the same height. Make 1 chain, skip the first stitch and work a single crochet into each stitch until the one chain loop at base has been reached.

8 Work a single crochet, chain and a single crochet into this 1-chain loop. Now continue in single crochet up other side of leaf until 3 stitches, including turning chain, remain unworked. Turn and leave these stitches.

9 Work a single crochet into each stitch all around leaf as before, working a single crochet, chain and a single crochet into the 1 chain space as before, until 3 stitches remain unworked on the other side of the leaf.

10 Now turn and repeat step 9, working 7 chains instead of 1 at the base of the leaf.

11 Now turn and make 1 chain. Work a single crochet into each stitch until you have reached the 7-chain loop at the base.

12 Now work 2 single crochets, 5 chains, 3 single crochets, 5 chains, 3 single crochets, 5 chains and 2 single crochets all into this loop.

13 Complete the leaf by working up the other side of the leaf until 3 stitches remain unworked and then fasten off the yarn.

14 Here are three leaves worked in a fine crochet cotton with a No. 10 (1.00mm) steel hook and grouped together to make a spray.

Fred Mancini

Shamrock

The shamrock is made very simply by working 3 large loops to form the basic shape, followed by working single crochets into each loop.

1 Make 16 chains. Work a single crochet into the first of these chains. Now make 15 more chains and work another single crochet into the last single crochet for the 2nd loop. Make the 3rd loop in the same way.

2 Now work 22 single crochets into each of these 3 loops, joining the last stitch to the first with a slip stitch.

3 Make 1 chain. Skip the first stitch and work a single crochet into each stitch all the way around, skipping the first and last stitch in each petal to draw them together.

4 Make the stem by working 25 chains, then turn and work a single crochet into the 3rd and every following chain back to the beginning.

5 Complete the stem by working a slip stitch into the first stitch of the next petal and fasten off the yarn. You will find it necessary to pin the motif out to the correct shape and press it with a damp cloth and hot iron so that it lies flat.

Working over a cord

Pattern directions may sometimes tell you to work part, or all, of a motif over a piece of cord so that you obtain a raised or ridged effect. Either you can use three or four strands of crochet cotton twisted together to make the cord (your directions will usually tell you how many strands to use), or you can use one strand of a thicker crochet cotton in a matching shade.

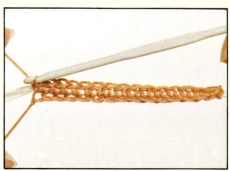

1 Once you have worked the foundation chain or reached the point where the cord is to be introduced, hold the cord— shown here in a contrasting color for clarity—at the back of the work in the left hand. Now work into the chain and over the cord at the same time.

2 Turn at the end of the row and hold the cord at the back of the work once more, then work back along the row and over the cord at the same time. Make sure that the cord passes through the stitches evenly when working more than 1 row.

3 Your directions may tell you how to work over the cord only—usually to form a loop at the base of a flower or leaf—and in this case you should hold the cord away from the main section and work in single crochet along the cord as neatly as possible.

4 To resume the pattern hold the cord at the back of the main section once more and continue to work into the stitches and over the cord as before.

5 Once the motif has been completed, trim the cord as close to the stitches as possible so that it remains hidden. Here is a single leaf worked over a cord in a matching color to obtain the ridged effect. Full instructions for the leaf are given on pages 16 and 17.

Fred Mancini

Stitch Wise

Triple leaf

Make 16 chains. From now on, work over a cord or 4 strands of the same yarns as shown on page 18.
1st row 1sc into 3rd ch from hook, 1sc into each ch until 1ch remains unworked, 5sc into last ch, 1sc into each ch along other side of foundation ch, 3sc over cord only, work into back loop only of each stitch from now on, 1sc into each sc to within 4sc from center sc at tip of leaf, turn.
2nd row 1ch, skip first sc, 1sc into each sc to within center sc of 3sc group worked on cord only, 3sc into center sc, 1sc into each sc on other side to within 4sc from center sc at tip of leaf. Turn.
3rd row 1ch, skip 1sc, 1sc into each sc to within center of 3sc group at base, 3sc into center sc, 1sc into each sc on other side to within last 3sc. Turn.
4th to 6th rows As 3rd row.
Fasten off.
Make 2 more leaves in same way, then sew sides of leaves together to form triple leaf.

Single rose

Make 6 chains and join into a circle with a sl st.
1st round 1ch to count as first sc, 11sc into circle, join with a sl st to first ch.
2nd round 7ch, skip first sc, 1dc into next sc, *5ch, skip 1sc, 1dc into next sc, rep from * to end of round, omitting last dc, join last ch to 3rd of first 7ch with a sl st.
3rd round Work (1sc, 1hdc, 5dc, 1hdc, 1sc) into each 5ch loop, join last sc to first with a sl st. Fasten off. 6 petals in all. To make a stem do not fasten off at end of last round but work number of chains required for stem, turn and work a sc into 3rd and every foll ch to end. Join with a sl st to next st on next petal. Fasten off.

19

Motifs for lace vest

These motifs can be sewn on the vest featured in course 47 on page 7. Attach them at random or position them according to your own design.

Materials
The 28 motifs used took
2oz (50g) of a fine pearl cotton

Shamrock
Using No. 0 (2.00mm) hook make 16ch.
1st row 1sc into 16th ch from hook,

15ch, 1sc into same ch, 15ch, 1sc into same ch.
2nd row Work 22sc into each loop.
3rd row Skipping first and last sc on each petal, work 1sc into each sc, sl st into first sc.
4th row Make 25ch for stem, 1sc into

3rd ch from hook, 1sc into each ch to end, sl st into first sc on petal. Fasten off.
Make 5 more motifs the same way.

Double rosebud motif
Using No. 0 (2.00mm) hook make 8ch, sl st into first ch to form a circle.
1st round 6ch, *1dc into circle, 3ch, rep from * 4 times more, sl st into 3rd of first 6ch. 6 spaces.
2nd round Into each sp work 1sc, 1hdc, 3dc, 1hdc and 1sc. 6 petals.
3rd round *5ch, inserting hook from back to front work 1sc around stem of next dc 2 rows below, rep from * to end, finishing 5ch, sl st into back of first ch.
4th round Into each sp work 1sc, 1hdc, 5dc, 1hdc and 1sc, sl st into first sc.
5th round *7ch, inserting hook from back to front work 1sc around stem of next sc 2 rows below, rep from * to end, finishing 7ch, sl st into back of first ch.
6th round Into each sp work 1sc, 1hdc, 7dc, 1hdc, and 1sc, sl st into first sc. Fasten off.
Make 5 more motifs the same way.

Single rose
Using No. 0 (2.00mm) hook make 6ch, sl st into first ch to form a circle.
1st round 1ch to count as first 2sc, work 11sc into circle, sl st into first ch.
2nd round 8ch, skip first 2sc, 1dc into next sc, *5ch, skip next sc, 1dc into next sc, rep from * all around, finishing 5ch, sl st into 3rd of the 8ch.
3rd round Into each loop work 1sc, 1hdc, 5dc, 1hdc and 1sc, sl st into base of first sc. Fasten off.
Make 5 more motifs the same way.

Single leaf
Using No. 0 (2.00mm) hook, make 16 ch.
1st row Working into one loop only, work 1sc into 3rd ch from hook, 1sc into each ch to within last ch, 3sc into last ch (tip of leaf), 1sc into each loop along other side of foundation ch, 1sc into same place as first sc.
2nd row Working into back loop only, work 1sc into each of next 11sc, turn.
3rd row 1ch, skip first sc, 1sc into each sc to within center sc at base of leaf, work 1sc, 1ch and 1sc all into center sc, 1sc into each sc along other side of leaf to within 4sc of center sc at tip of leaf, turn.
4th row 1ch, skip first sc, 1sc into each sc to within 1 ch sp, work 1sc, 1ch and 1sc all into sp, 1sc into each sc along other side of leaf to within last 3 sts, turn.
5th row As 4th.
6th row As 4th, but work 7ch at base of leaf instead of 1 ch, turn.
7th row 1ch, 1sc into each sc to within 7ch loop, work 2sc, 5ch, 3sc, 5ch, 3sc, 5ch and 2sc all into loop, 1sc into each sc along other side of leaf to within last 3 sts. Fasten off.
Work 9 more motifs the same way.

Crochet / COURSE 50

*Irish crochet medallions
*Rose medallion
*Joining the motifs
*Stitch Wise: more Irish crochet
*Pattern for a lacy bedspread

Irish crochet medallions

Now that you have learned how to work both the lace background patterns and some of the motifs used in Irish crochet, you can combine the two by working the motif first, followed by the lace pattern worked in ever-increasing circles around the central motif, to create square or circular medallions. These can then be sewn or crocheted together to make place mats, bedspreads, tablecloths and many other household items. Small medallions could be joined together in a strip and sewn to the edge of a petticoat or a child's dress for a pretty lace edging.

The technique for working these squares is very much the same as for working any square or circle in crochet. Once you have practiced working the rose medallion

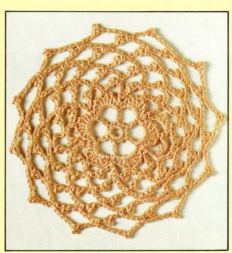

featured in the previous crochet course, you should have no difficulty in working any other Irish crochet medallion. Once you have learned how to work these squares, try experimenting with different motifs and lace patterns. For example, try combining the single rose on page 19, with the single picot mesh pattern on page 7, as shown here.

Like all Irish crochet patterns, these medallions look best worked in a cotton yarn with the appropriate hook (see Volume 8, page 23 for hook and yarn chart), so that the resulting lace is worked firmly and evenly and looks crisp.

Once the medallions have been finished, they should be pinned out and blocked to the correct size and shape.

Rose medallion

In this course we show you how to work the rose medallion with crown motifs featured in the beautiful bedspread in this course. To help you work the medallion, the first few rounds will be shown in the step-by-step photographs. For full details on how to complete the motif, refer to the instructions given in the bedspread pattern on page 27.

Our sample has been worked in a medium-weight crochet cotton using a No. 0 (2.00mm) steel hook so that you will be able to see clearly how each step has been worked. Once you have practiced with this relatively thick yarn, you should experiment with finer crochet cottons to see the superb results which can be achieved.

1 Work the double rosebud from the instructions given on page 21. Do not fasten off the yarn at the end of the last round. Now begin to work the background lace by working a single crochet into the first single crochet of the next petal.

2 Now make 4 chains, then work 1 single crochet into the 3rd chain from the hook for the first picot. Now work 5 chains followed by a single crochet into the 3rd of these chains from the hook for the 2nd picot.

3 Make 2 chains. Now work 1 single crochet into the center of the same petal. Steps 2 and 3 complete the first picot loop.

4 Repeat step 2 once more. Make 2 chains, then work 1 single crochet into the first single crochet in the next petal to complete the 2nd picot loop.

5 Continue to work picot loops all around the flower, working a single crochet alternately into the center of each petal and into the first single crochet of the next petal. Omit the last single crochet and join with a slip stitch to the first single crochet.

6 To continue working around the motif, slip stitch to the center of the first picot loop so that you start the next round between the first two picot points of the previous round.

7 Now make 1 chain to count as the first single crochet, followed by 8 chains. Now work 1 single crochet between the two picot points of the next loop. Turn and slip stitch back into this 8-chain loop to start the first crown motif.

8 Now work 3 chains to count as the first double, followed by 9 doubles into the 8-chain loop. Work a final double into the 1 chain worked at the beginning of the round.

9 Now turn so that you are working back along these 11 stitches. Make 4 chains to count as the first double and chain. Continue to work 1 double followed by 1 chain into every other stitch, working the last double into the top of first 3 chains at the start of the crown. (6 doubles.)

10 Now work 4 chains followed by a single crochet into the 3rd chain from the hook for a picot. Make 2 chains, then work a single crochet into the same 8-chain loop as the completed crown motif.

11 Now work 2 more picot loops as before, each time working the single crochet between the 2 picot points made in the previous round.

continued

Fred Mancini

23

12 Make 8 chains and work a single crochet between the next 2 picot points. Now repeat steps 7-10 once more for the 2nd crown, working the 11th double of first row into the single crochet worked at the beginning of the 8-chain loop.

13 Continue to work 2 picot loops followed by a crown, twice more, to complete the round. Finish with 2 picot loops, omitting the last single crochet but joining the last chain to the first with a slip stitch.

14 Work alternate rounds of plain picot loops and crown motif and picot loops until the square is the required size. Always complete a square with a plain picot loop round and remember to work extra loops on each side of the square to increase the size. For detailed instructions see page 27.

Stitch Wise

Lace flower

Make 6ch. Join into a circle with a sl st.
1st round 1ch to count as first sc, work 7sc into circle. Join with a sl st to first ch. Beg first petal.
1st row 3ch, work 1sc into same place as joining sl st, (3ch, 1sc into same place as last sc) twice. Turn.
2nd row 4ch, *work 1sc into next loop, 3ch, rep from * once more, 1sc into next loop. Turn.
3rd-5th rows 4ch, *1sc into next loop, 3ch, rep from * once more, 1sc into next loop. Turn.
Skip next sc on center circle. Rejoin yarn to next sc and work a 2nd petal in same way as before. Work 2 more petals in same way.
Edging
1st round Rejoin yarn to sc before first petal. Work 1 round sc around each

petal, working 2sc into each corner to keep petals flat. Join with a sl st to first sc.
2nd round 1ch to count as first sc, skip first sc, 1sc into each sc to first corner of first petal, 4ch, sl st into top of last sc – 1 picot –, 1sc into each sc to center of first petal, 1 picot into next sc, 1sc into each sc to 2nd corner of first petal, 1 picot into next sc, 1sc into each sc to base of first petal. Work 1sc into first sc of 2nd petal and then cont to work around each petal in same way. Join with a sl st to first st of first petal. Fasten off.

Single rose center
Make 14ch. Sl st to first ch to form a circle.
1st round Work (1sc, 1hdc, 5dc, 1hdc) 4 times into circle. Join with a sl st to first sc. Fasten off.
Sew single rose to center of four petals to complete flower.

Decorative leaf

Make 21 ch.
1st row 1sc into 3rd ch from hook, 1sc into each ch to last ch, 3sc into last ch. Cont to work along other side of foundation ch, 1sc into each ch to end. Turn.
2nd row Work into back loop only of each st, 1ch to count as first sc, skip first st, 1sc into each sc to within 3sc group at tip of leaf, 2sc into each of next 3sc, 1sc into each sc to end, working last sc into turning ch. Turn.
3rd row 4ch, *skip next 3sc, 1sc into next sc, 4ch, rep from * 3 times more, ** skip 2sc, 1sc into next sc, 4ch, rep from **twice more, *** skip 3sc, 1sc into next sc, 4ch, rep from *** twice more, 1sc into turning chain. Fasten off.
Here we show 3 leaves sewn together at the base.

Double primrose

Make 15 ch. Join into a circle with a sl st.
1st round *6ch, 1sc into circle, rep from *4 times more, omitting last sc and

Joining the motifs

It is important when joining Irish crochet medallions to match the pattern, so that the fabric remains light and lacy.

You can either sew the motifs together, catching the picots on each side of the squares with a small stitch to hold them together as shown here, or crochet them together by working the last round of the second and subsequent squares at the same time as joining it to the side of the previous square. Your instructions will tell you how the squares should be joined, but the simplest way is to slip stitch into a corresponding picot point on the first square while working the picot loop of the second square.

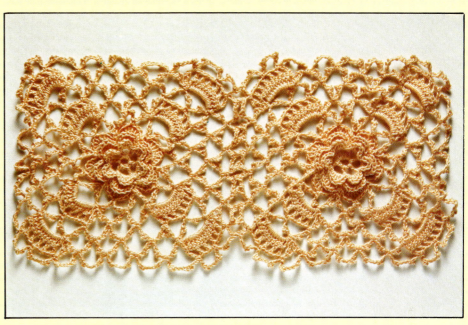

Fred Mancini

joining with a sl st to first ch.

2nd round Into each 6ch loop work (1sc, 1hdc, 1dc, 8tr, 1dc, 1hdc, 1sc). Join with a sl st to sp formed by original ring at base of primrose.

3rd round Into each space at base of 2nd round work (1hdc, 5dc, 1hdc). Fasten off. To make an unusual flower work several decorative leaves and sew them together at base of each leaf. Then sew a double primrose to the center of these leaves, as shown here.

Flower with seven petals

Petal

Make 17 ch.

1st row 1dc into 7th ch from hook, *2ch, skip next ch, 1dc into next ch, rep from * to end. 6 spaces. Turn.

2nd row 1ch to count as first sc, 2sc into first sp, *3sc into next sp, rep from * 3 times more, 10sc into next sp, cont to

work along other side of foundation ch, 3sc into each sp to end. Turn.

3rd row 3ch, skip first sc, 1dc into each sc all around petal, working last dc into turning chain. Turn.

4th row 1ch to count as first sc, skip first st, 1sc into each of next 3sc, 3ch, sl st into last sc worked—1 picot—, * 1sc into each of next 4sc, 1 picot, rep from * to last 4 sts, 1sc into each of next 3 sts, 1sc into turning chain. Fasten off. Make 6 more petals in same way. Sew 7 petals together so that they overlap at base as shown here.

Flower center

1st round Make 10ch and join into a circle with a sl st.

2nd round Join in a cord (see page 18), using 4 strands of same yarn or 1 strand of thicker yarn, 1ch, work 21sc into

circle working over cord. Join with a sl st to first ch. 22sc.

Continue to work over the cord until the flower center has been completed and work into back loop only of each st from now on.

3rd round. Work 10sc over cord only. Turn. *1ch, skip first st, 1sc into each sc to base of petal, **, 1sc into each of next 2sc on center round. Turn. (1 petal completed.) 1ch, skip 2 sts, 1sc into each of next 3 sts, 7sc over cord only, turn and rep from * to base of 2nd petal. Continue to work each petal in same way working from ** each time, until 11 petals in all have been completed. Join with a sl st to base of first petal. Fasten off. Join base of last petal to base of first petal with a few invisible stitches. Sew this flower to center of 7 completed petals to finish flower.

Lacy bedspread

Irish crochet shamrocks and roses surrounded by picot lace form the motifs of this dreamy bedspread. Made in cotton yarn, it will enhance any bedroom, whether the decor is traditional or modern.

Sizes
Twin bed 36×60in (90×150cm).
Double bed 54×60in (135×150cm).

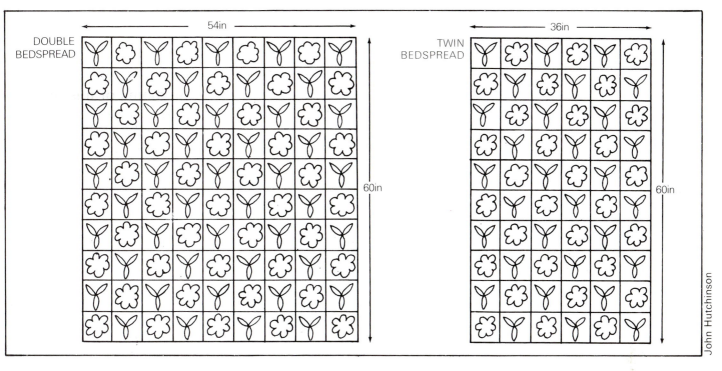

DOUBLE BEDSPREAD — 54in — 60in

TWIN BEDSPREAD — 36in — 60in

John Hutchinson

Materials
A medium-weight crochet cotton
Twin size bed 13×2oz (50g) balls
Double size bed 20×2oz (50g) balls
Size B (2.50mm) crochet hook

Gauge
One motif measures 6in (15cm) square worked on size B (2.50mm) hook.

Shamrock motif
Using size B (2.50mm) hook make 16ch.
1st row 1sc into 16th ch from hook, 15ch, 1sc into same ch as last sc, 15ch, 1sc into same ch as last sc to complete base for shamrock shape.
2nd round Working over a cord or 4 strands of the same yarn, work 25sc into each loop. Cut off cord.
3rd round 1ch, skip first sc, 1sc into each sc in each loop to complete the shamrock.
4th round Sl st into each of next 4 sts, ** 1sc into next sc, *4ch, 1sc into 3rd ch from hook—picot formed—, 5ch, 1sc into 3rd ch from hook, 2ch—a picot loop made—, skip next 4sc, 1sc into next sc, rep from * twice more, work 1 picot loop, skip next 4sc of next leaf of shamrock, rep from **, ending with 1 picot loop, join with a sl st to first sc. 12 picot loops made.
5th round Sl st to center of first picot loop (between picots), 1sc into same loop, *8ch, 1sc between picots of next picot loop, turn, sl st into loop just made, 3ch, 9dc into same loop, 1dc into next sc, 4ch, turn, skip first 2dc, 1dc into next dc, (1ch, skip next dc, 1dc into next dc) 3 times, 1ch, skip next dc, 1dc into top of 3ch, 4ch, 1sc into 3rd ch from hook, 2ch, 1sc into same loop to complete first crown motif, (4ch, 1sc into 3rd ch from hook, 5ch, 1sc into 3rd ch from hook, 2ch, 1sc between

picots of next picot loop) twice, rep from *to end, omitting sc at end of last rep, join with a sl st to first sc.
6th round Sl st up side of dc and into each of the next 3ch up side of crown motif, 1sc into first sp of first crown motif, *4ch, 1sc into 3rd ch from hook, 5ch, 1sc into 3rd ch from hook, 2ch, skip next sp, 1sc into next sp, 4ch, 1sc into 3rd ch from hook, 5ch, 1sc into 3rd ch from hook, 2ch, skip next 2 sps, 1sc into next loop at edge of crown motif, (4ch, 1sc into 3rd ch from hook, 5ch, 1sc into 3rd ch from hook, 2ch, 1sc between picots of next loop) twice, 4ch, 1sc into 3rd ch from hook, 5ch, 1sc into 3rd ch from hook, 2ch, 1sc into first sp of next crown motif, rep from * omitting 1sc at end of last rep, join with a sl st to first sc.
7th round Sl st to center of first picot loop, 1sc into same loop, *8ch, 1sc between picots of next loop, turn, work 1 crown motif as before into this 8ch loop, (4ch, 1sc into 3rd ch from hook, 5ch, 1sc into 3rd ch from hook, 2ch, 1sc between picots of next loop) 4 times, rep from * omitting sc at end of last rep, join with a sl st to first sc.
8th round Sl st up side of dc and next 3ch of first crown motif, 1sc into first sp, *4ch, 1sc into 3rd ch from hook, 5ch, 1sc into 3rd ch from hook, 2ch, skip next sp, 1sc into next sp, 4ch, 1sc into 3rd ch from hook, 5ch, 1sc into 3rd ch from hook, 2ch, skip next 2 sps, 1sc into next loop, (4ch, 1sc into 3rd ch from hook, 5ch 1sc into 3rd ch from hook, 2ch, 1sc between picots of next loop) 4 times, 4ch, 1sc into 3rd ch from hook, 5ch, 1sc into 3rd ch from hook, 2ch, 1sc into first sp of next crown motif, rep from * omitting sc at end of last rep, join with a sl st to first sc.
Fasten off.

Rose motif
Using size B (2.50mm) hook make 8ch, sl st into first ch to form a circle.
1st round 6ch, *1dc into circle, 3ch, rep from * 4 times more, sl st into 3rd of first 6ch. 6 sps.
2nd round into each sp work 1sc, 1hdc, 3dc, 1hdc and 1sc. 6 petals.
3rd round *5ch, inserting hook from back to front work 1sc around next dc on first round, rep from * ending with 5ch, join with a sl st to first ch.
4th round into each sp work 1sc, 1hdc, 5dc, 1hdc and 1sc.
5th round *7ch, 1sc into next sc on 3rd round working around stem as before, rep from * ending with 7ch, join with a sl st to first ch.
6th round Into each sp work 1sc, 1hdc, 7dc, 1hdc and 1sc. This completes the rose.
7th round 1ch, 1sc into first sc of next petal, *4ch, 1sc into 3rd ch from hook—picot formed—, 5ch, 1sc into 3rd ch from hook, 2ch, 1sc into center dc of same petal—picot loop formed—, 4ch, 1sc into 3rd ch from hook, 5ch, 1sc into 3rd ch from hook, 2ch, 1sc into first sc of next petal, rep from * omitting sc at end of last rep, join with a sl st to first sc.
8th–11th rounds As 5th–8th rounds of shamrock motif. Fasten off.
For twin size bed make 30 motifs in each design.
For double size bed make 45 motifs in each design.
To finish
Alternate the motifs and join together by sewing the two picot loops from the center ch loop, skip 3 picots and join next 2 picots (on both sides).
For twin size bed join 6 by 10 motifs.
For double size bed join 9 by 10 motifs.

Glasses with class

Protect your glasses with a smart needlepoint case worked in stripes of satin stitch.

Paul Williams

Finished size
6½ × 3¼in (16.5 × 8cm).

Materials
Piece of No. 14-mesh single thread canvas, 8 × 5in (20 × 13cm)
One skein of tapestry yarn in three contrasting or harmonizing colors
⅛yd (.1m) of 36in (90cm)-wide corduroy to match one of the yarn colors
No. 22 tapestry needle
Piece of heavyweight interfacing 6½ × 3¼in (16.5 × 8cm)
Matching thread

1 From corduroy cut out one piece 7½ × 4in (18.5 × 10cm) for back. Cut out one piece 14 × 4in (35 × 10cm) for lining.
2 For the case front work rows of satin stitch over six horizontal and two vertical threads across the canvas, starting about ¾in (2cm) from the top and left-hand edges. Work each row from left to right, alternating colors.
3 Work the stripes on the canvas until the stitching measures 6½ × 3¼in (16.5 × 8cm). Press with steam iron and pull into shape. (If work is badly distorted, block it as instructed in Volume 1, page 72.)
4 Place corduroy backing and needlepoint front together, right sides facing. Pin, baste and stitch around the edges, right beside needlepoint, leaving one end open. Trim canvas to match fabric. Turn case right side out.
5 Fold lining in half widthwise, right sides together. Pin, baste and stitch both long edges to form a bag slightly smaller than the outer case. Insert lining into case, wrong sides together.
6 Trim piece of interfacing until it fits inside the case between the lining and back of the case.
7 Turn in the top raw edges of case and lining. Slip stitch together around top.

*Chain-looped edgings
*Double-looped edging
*Single-looped edging
*Edging a jacket or cardigan
*Pattern for a shaggy jerkin

Chain-looped edgings

Crocheted looped edgings make attractive trimmings for garments and household items. Thick ones can be used to give a luxurious look to a coat or jacket; a single row of loops makes an authentic-looking fringe for a western-style jerkin.
A very simple looped edging can be made by working a length of chain after every stitch, so that once the next stitch has been worked the chain will form a loop at the base of the fabric. The basic method of making the loop is shown at right, followed by four chain looped edgings using different types of yarn, including crochet cotton and mohair. Experiment with these and other yarns to see the variety of effects you can create.

For a narrow edging work a row of single crochet the length you need for your edging. On the following row work the first stitch, then a length of chain twice the length of the completed loop. When the 2nd single crochet is worked, the length of chain forms a single loop as shown here. Work loops of the same length all along the row.

A 2-ply yarn was used for this sample. Work a row of single crochet, followed by a 2nd row of single crochet working 20 chains after each stitch in the 2nd row to form the loops. Start the row with 20 chains and skip the first stitch in the normal way. Complete the row with a single crochet, worked into the turning chain for the best results.

Here a row of bobbles (see Volume 5, page 10) has been worked between four single crochet rows to form the heading, before the single crochet loop row is worked.

This sample has been worked in a fine mohair yarn, with two rows of half doubles worked before the loop row. 30 chains have been worked for each loop. For a wider heading work four or five rows of half doubles before working the loops.

This pretty cotton edging has been made by working 1 row of single crochet followed by a row of doubles and 2-chain spaces. Skip 2 stitches between each double to form the spaces and work the last double into the turning chain. When you work the loop row, work a single crochet into each chain and double worked in the previous row with 20 chains in each loop. Then thread ribbon through the spaces for a delicate edging.

Double-looped edging

One of the most popular methods of making loops in crochet is to wind the yarn around the fingers of the left hand or a piece of stiff cardboard to make the loops as you work the edging. The loops are formed at the back of the work, so the loop row must always be worked on the wrong side of the fabric so that the loops fall on the right side of the work. This method is most frequently used to make a bulky edging, since several layers of loops can be worked to make a thick border.

1 Work a row of single crochet to the desired length. Make 1 chain and insert the hook into the 2nd stitch. Wind the yarn twice around the first three fingers of the left hand and taking yarn around the front and then back of fingers each time.

2 For a shorter loop, wind the yarn around two fingers. For a single loop, wind the yarn only once around the fingers.

3 Bring the working strand of yarn up behind the fingers and lay it across the top of the first finger and across the first two strands of yarn.

4 Now insert the hook under all three strands of yarn, taking the hook from left to right, and draw all three strands through the stitch being worked. Drop the loops. By taking all three strands through the stitch you make sure that the loops are locked in place firmly.

5 Wind the yarn over the hook and complete the single crochet in the normal way to complete the first loop stitch. Here is the loop worked on the right side of the edging.

6 Continue to work a loop stitch into every stitch across the row, working a single crochet into the top of the turning chain only to maintain a straight edge.

7 This sample shows the completed row on the right side of the work, with all the loops hanging down, knotted firmly in place.

8 For a thicker edging, work another single crochet row followed by another loop row. Several layers of loops can be worked for a really thick edging as shown here.

Single-looped edging

Here is a simple method of working the loops over a piece of cardboard. In this case the loops will be made from a single strand of yarn, instead of a double strand as shown in the previous method.

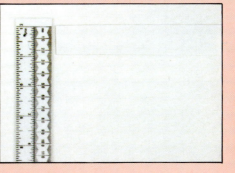

1 Cut a strip of cardboard the right width for the length of loop needed. Ours measures 1in (2.5cm) and is easy to manage. You could use a much wider one for really long loops, but you may find that it is difficult to hold a wide piece of cardboard and work at the same time.

2 Work a row of single crochet. Turn and make 1 chain. Draw a loop of yarn through the 2nd stitch. Hold the cardboard behind the work and wind the yarn around it from front to back.

3 Now take the working end of the yarn over the top of the cardboard and draw it through the two loops on the hook to complete the loop stitch. Complete the row by working a loop stitch into every single crochet until the row has been completed.

4 Withdraw the cardboard after all the loops have been completed. Here we show you the right side of the work with the loops worked across the row.

5 For a wider edging work several rows of loops with a row of single crochet worked between each loop. Alternatively, work a single row of loops at the bottom of several rows of single crochet to make the heading wider, as shown here.

Edging a jacket or cardigan

When working a looped edging to go around a jacket or cardigan it is a good idea to decide how you want the loops to fall before starting to make the border. If you work the edging in one continuous strip to go all the way around the lower edge, up the left front, around the neck and down the right front, you will find the loops at the lower edge hang down and the loops sewn on the front edges lie at right angles to the garment, as shown on the near right.
To make sure that the loops all hang the same way, work the edges separately, so that the front borders are worked as a narrow band which can then be sewn on the front of the garment. Then the loops will hang downward, as shown on the far right.

Mike Berend

Shaggy jerkin

Wear this stylish jerkin, with its simple shaping and looped edging, as an extra layer over shirts and sweaters.

Size
To fit 34in (86cm) bust.
Length, 25in (63cm).

Materials
- 15oz (400g) of a heavy-weight bouclé (A)
- 13oz (350g) of a knitting worsted (B)
- Sizes H and I (5.00 and 6.00mm) crochet hooks

Gauge
11hdc and 8 rows to 4in (10cm) on size I (6.00mm) hook, with A.
14 sts and 12 rows to 4in (10cm) over loop st on size H (5.00mm) hook, with B.

Back
Using size I (6.00mm) hook and A, make 53ch.
Base row 1hdc into 3rd ch from hook, 1hdc into each ch to end. Turn. 52hdc.
Patt row 2ch to count as first hdc, 1hdc into each hdc to end, 1hdc into turning ch. Turn.
Rep the patt row until work measures 13in (33cm); end with a WS row.
Cut off yarn.
Shape armholes
Next row Skip first 5hdc, rejoin yarn to next hdc, 2ch, work in patt until 5 sts remain unworked. Turn. 42 hdc.
Cont straight until armhole measures 8in (20cm); end with a WS row.
Shape neck
Next row Work in patt across first 8 sts, turn and cont on these 8 sts for 2in (5cm).
Fasten off.
Skip center 26 sts, rejoin yarn to next st and patt to end. Finish as for first side.

Left front
Using size I (6.00mm) hook and A, make 21ch. Work base row and patt row as for back. 20 hdc. Cont in patt until work measures same as back to armhole; end with a RS row.
Shape armhole
Next row Patt to last 5 sts, turn. 15 hdc. Cont straight until armhole measures 4in (10cm); end at armhole edge.
Shape neck
Next row Patt across first 8 sts, turn and cont on these 8 sts until armhole measures same as back to shoulder. Fasten off.

Right front
Work as for left front, reversing shaping.

Lower border
Using size H (5.00mm) hook and B, make 117ch.
1st row 1sc into 3rd ch from hook, 1sc into each ch to end. Turn. 116sc.
2nd row 1ch, *insert hook into next st, wind yarn twice around first 3 fingers of left hand (see Double-looped edging, page 30), insert hook under all 3 strands of yarn and draw through st, yo and draw through 2 loops on hook—called 1 loop st—, rep from * to end, 1 sc into turning chain. Turn.
3rd row 1ch to count as first st, skip first st, 1sc into each st, working last sc into turning chain. Turn. Rep 2nd and 3rd rows once more, then 2nd row again. Fasten off

Front borders (make 2)
Using size H (5.00mm) hook and B, make 75ch. Work border as for lower border.

Back neck border
Using size H (5.00mm) hook and B, make 34ch. Work as for lower border.

Front neck borders (make 2)
Using size H (5.00mm) hook and B, make 30ch. Work as for lower border.

Armhole borders (make 2)
Using size H (5.00mm) hook and B, make 71ch. Work border as for lower border.

To finish
Do not press. Join shoulder seams. Sew armhole borders to armholes with loops lying outward. Sew ends of borders to bound-off sts at armholes at each side. Join sides. Sew on bottom edge with loops lying downward. Sew on back neck border with ends to sides of neck shaping. Sew on front neck edges with loops lying inward, easing border around front corners and sewing ends at back to back borders. Sew on front edges, starting at top of neck borders, with loops lying toward center front on each side.

Chris Harvey

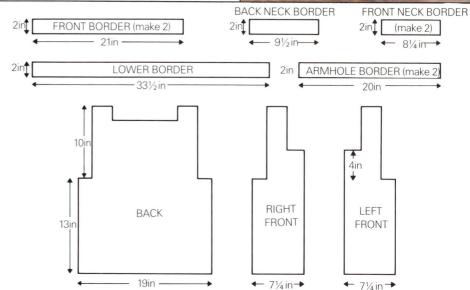

Knitting / COURSE 47

Knitting with sequins

Sequins, like beads, can be added to knitting using the technique called bead knitting given in Volume 10, page 53. But in bead knitting it is necessary to pass the beads or sequins through the stitch (which can be more tedious for sequins than for beads, as sequins are a more awkward shape) you may prefer to use another technique for sequins traditionally known as beaded knitting. In beaded knitting the bead or sequin is placed between stitches instead of on them. This can be done on most forms of knitting, including stockinette stitch, garter stitch and openwork

patterns. Sequins are available in a wide variety of colors, shapes and sizes. There are three things to consider when choosing them. First, the type of sequin may determine the technique. For instance, large sequins with a hole close to the side will hang downward only if you use bead knitting—and the stitches must be large enough for the sequin to pass through. Equally important is matching the yarn and the sequin so that the yarn passes easily through the eye of the sequin. And finally, make sure that the sequins can be dry cleaned.

Sequins on stockinette stitch

In beaded knitting, the bead or sequin is most commonly placed on the horizontal bar either between two purl stitches or between a purl stitch and a knit stitch. This bar holds the bead or sequin forward and keeps it from slipping to the back of the work.

Before beginning to knit, thread the sequins onto the yarn following the threading instructions for beads given in Volume 10, page 51. The method illustrated here is suitable for sprinkling beads over the knitted fabric.

1 Knit to the position of the sequin, leaving at least two edge stitches plain. Bring the yarn forward as if to purl the next stitch.

2 Slide the sequin up close to the work and then purl the next stitch. Continue knitting until the position of the next sequin is reached. Purl the return row.

Sequins on garter stitch

With garter stitch, both solid sequin motifs and solid sequin fabrics can be produced. The sequins lie between two purl stitches. The instructions show the sequins knitted into every other row, but sequin motifs can be made by applying the same principle—with the garter stitch being introduced for the motif only and the background knitted in stockinette stitch. When knitting motifs you will have to follow a design chart. If there are several colors of sequins in the pattern, remember to follow the chart for threading in sequence (see Volume 10, page 52).

1 The sequins are added when knitting the WS rows. First knit two edge stitches.

2 Then slide the sequin up to the back of your knitting. As you are on a WS row, the front of your work is facing away from you.

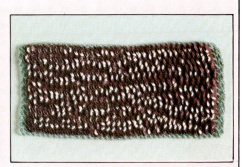

3 Knit the next stitch and continue adding a sequin after each stitch until you reach the last two stitches, which are worked without sequins.

4 On the next row (the RS row) the sequins will be facing you. Knit all RS rows without sequins. This prevents the work from curling.

5 If the sequins are added in every other row of garter stitch and if the individual stitches are not too large the surface will be entirely covered with sequins.

Sequins on openwork patterns

Sequins are an effective adornment on lace patterns, especially lace edgings. The eyelet provides the site for the sequins as they are easily introduced when the yarn over is made to form the hole. If the eyelets are spaced far enough apart, a sequin can be added with every yarn over. It is best to test a small sample of a lace pattern with sequins first as the sequins may tend to hang to the back of the work instead of to the front. Lace patterns with a garter stitch ground alleviate this problem because there is no back or front.

Frederick Mancini

1 Work in pattern to the position of the eyelet. Take the yarn forward and slide the sequin up to the work. Then, keeping the yarn forward insert the needle into the next stitch and knit it.

2 The sequin will now lie on the side of the work facing you at the base of the new loop on the needle. In the next row this new loop is worked the same way as the other stitches.

Samples of knitting with sequins

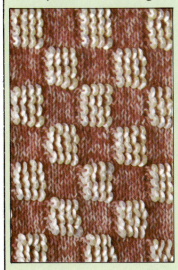

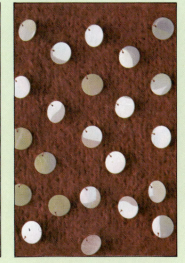

Check pattern

Sequins with slip stitch

Sequins on mohair

Chevron pattern

Stuart Macleod

Vest, bow tie and evening bag

Add sparkle to evenings out with this sequinned set. You could wear the vest by itself or over a silky shirt. Add extra dash with a matching bow tie and evening bag.

Sizes

Vest 32[34:36]in (83[87:92]cm) bust.
Length, 17¼[17¾:18¼]in (44[45:46]cm).
Bag 4in (10cm) × 7in (18cm).
Note Directions for larger sizes are in brackets [ ]; if there is only one set of figures it applies to all sizes.

Materials

Sport yarn
  Vest 6oz (150g)
  Approximately 2,000 sequins
  5 buttons
  Bow tie 1oz (25g)
  500 sequins
  Narrow elastic to fit around neck
  Bag 2oz (50g)
  500 sequins
  10in (25cm) × 7in (18cm) lining
  10in (25cm) × 7in (18cm) interfacing
  1 button
  1 pair No. 5 (4mm) knitting needles

Gauge

20 sts and 28 rows to 4in (10cm) on No. 5 (4mm) needles.
The sequins are threaded onto the yarn before beginning to knit the garment. If more are needed, break off yarn, thread on sequins, then continue as before. The sequins are always purled into the stitch. The yarn is brought forward, the sequin slid into place so that it lies flat against the work, then the next stitch is purled. In the pattern, this process is called sequin 1 or seq 1.

Vest

Back

Using No. 5 (4mm) needles cast on 69 [75:81] sts. K 10 rows. Beg sequin patt.
1st row (RS) *K2, seq 1, rep from * to

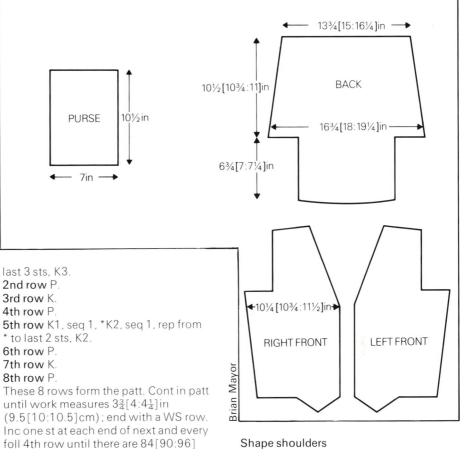

last 3 sts, K3.
2nd row P.
3rd row K.
4th row P.
5th row K1, seq 1, *K2, seq 1, rep from * to last 2 sts, K2.
6th row P.
7th row K.
8th row P.
These 8 rows form the patt. Cont in patt until work measures 3¾[4:4¼]in (9.5[10:10.5]cm); end with a WS row. Inc one st at each end of next and every foll 4th row until there are 84[90:96] sts. Cont straight until work measures 10½[10¾:11]in (26.5[27:27.5]cm); end with a WS row.

Shape armholes

Bind off 16 sts at beg of next 2 rows. 52[58:64] sts. Cont straight until armhole measures 6¾[7:7¼]in (17.5[18:18.5]cm); end with a WS row.

Shape shoulders

Bind off 8 sts at beg of next 4 rows.
Bind off.

Right front

Using No. 5 (4mm) needles cast on 2 sts.
Next row K.
Working in garter st (every row K), inc one st at each end of every row until there are 24 sts.**
Next row Cast on 19[22:25], then K30 [33:36], P2, K11. 43[46:49] sts.
Next row K.
Next row K28[31:34], P6, K9.
Next row K11, seq 1, K2, seq 1, K to end.
Next row K26[29:32], P10, K7.
Next row K.
Next row K24[27:30], P14, K5.
Next row K7, seq 1, (K2, seq 1) 4 times, K to end.
Next row K22[25:28], P18, K3.
Next row K.
Next row K20[23:26], P22, K1.
Next row *K2, seq 1, rep from * to last st, K1.
Next row P.
Next row K.
Next row P.
Beg sequin patt.
1st row K1, seq 1, *K2, seq 1, rep from * to last 2 sts, K2.
2nd, 4th, 6th, 8th rows P.
3rd row K.
5th row *K2, seq 1, rep from * to last st, K1.
7th row K.
These 8 rows form the patt. Cont in patt until work measures 6in (15cm) from

Brian Mayor

Stuart Macleod

point of V; end with a WS row.
Inc one st at end of next and every foll 4th row until there are 51[54:57] sts.
Cont straight until work measures 10[10¼:10½]in (25.5[26:26.5]cm) from point of V; end with a WS row.

Shape front edge

Dec one st at beg of next and every foll 4th row until side seam measures same as back to armhole shaping; end with a RS row.

Shape armhole

Bind off 16 sts at beg of next row.
Cont to dec one st at front edge on every 4th row until 19[22:25] sts rem.

Shape shoulder

Bind off 8 sts at beg of next and foll alternate row. Work 1 row. Bind off.

Left front

Work as for right front to **.
Next row Cast on 19[22:25] sts, then K to end of row. 43[46:49] sts.
Next row K11, P2, K30[33:36].
Next row K.
Next row K9, P6, K28[31:34].
Next row K28[31:34], seq 1, K2, seq 1, K11.
Next row K7, P10, K26[29:32].
Next row K.
Next row K5, P14, K24[27:30].
Next row K23[26:29], seq 1, (K2, seq 1) 4 times, K7.
Next row K3, P18, K22[25:28].
Next row K.
Next row K1, P22, K20[23:26].
Next row K1, *seq 1, K2, rep from * to end.
Next row P.
Next row K.
Next row P.
Beg sequin patt.
1st row *K2, seq 1, rep from * to last st, K1.
2nd, 4th, 6th, 8th rows P.
3rd row K.
5th row K1, *seq 1, K2, rep from * to end.
7th row K.
These 8 rows form the patt. Complete as for right front, reversing shaping.

Front border

Using No. 5 (4mm) needles cast on 8 sts.
K 2 rows.
1st buttonhole row K3, bind off 2, K to end.
2nd buttonhole row K3, cast on 2, K3.
Cont in garter st, making a total of 5 buttonholes 2in (5cm) apart, until border is 27½in (70cm) long, when slightly stretched. Bind off.

Armhole borders (alike)

Using No. 5 (4mm) needles cast on 8 sts.
Work in garter st until border measures 23½in (60cm) slightly stretched. Bind off.

To finish

Join shoulders easing front onto back.
Join side seams. Sew on borders and buttons.

Evening bag

Using No. 5 (4mm) needles cast on 36 sts.
K 10 rows. Beg sequin patt.
1st row K6, P24, K6.
2nd row K6, *K2, seq 1, rep from * to last 6 sts, K6.
3rd row As 1st.
4th row K.
5th row As 1st.
6th row K7, seq 1, *K2. seq 1, rep from * to last 7 sts, K7.
7th row As 1st.
8th row K.
These 8 rows form the patt. Cont in patt until work measures 9in (23cm) from beg. K 10 rows. Bind off.

To finish

Following diagrams, interface and line bag, then fold and join side seams.
Sew on button. Make button loop.

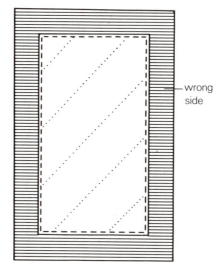

Cut a piece of interfacing 8in (20cm) × 4½ (11cm). Sew to WS of bag section.

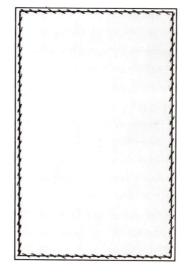

Brian Mayor

Cut lining fabric 10½ (27cm) × 7in (18cm). Turn under ⅜in (1cm) all around; sew to WS of interfaced bag.

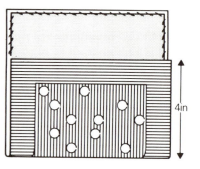

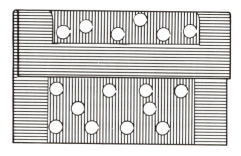

Measure up 4in (10cm), mark line across bag; fold along line. Sew sides.

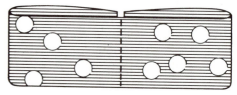

Fold down flap. Press lightly with a damp cloth. Make button loop and sew on button.

Bow tie

Main piece

Using No. 5 (4mm) needles cast on 9 sts.
Work in garter st for 2¼in (6cm). Cont in sequin patt as for bag, omitting edge sts until work measures 8in (20cm); end with a WS row. Work in garter st for 2¼in (6cm). Bind off.

Center piece

Using No. 5 (4mm) needles cast on 5 sts.
Work in garter st for 2in (5cm). Bind off.

To finish

Join short ends of main piece, gathering slightly. Fold center piece around center of main piece and join short ends at back. Sew on elastic, making a loop to fit around neck.

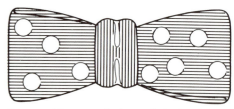

Join the short ends of the main tie section.

Cover with second piece of tie, joining ends behind. Attach elastic.

Knitting / COURSE 48

Making mock pleats

There are a number of different types of knitted pleats. Basically they are all quite simple and it is easy to use them in a skirt design of your own adaptation. Either finish the waist of the skirt with a herringbone casing sewn over a piece of elastic, or make a separate waistband and thread the elastic through (see Volume 6, page 57 and Volume 10, page 33 for details).

When making a skirt, remember to use a yarn that will retain its shape without drooping; pure wool crepe is ideal for this purpose. Most weights of yarn are suitable for skirts, although a 4-ply sport yarn is preferable as it is less bulky than knitting worsted, for example.

The mock pleats shown here are the easiest and most economical form of pleating. Work the two pattern rows to make the fabric pleat automatically.

Width around hem	32in
Stitch gauge	25 sts=4in
No. of sts around hem	$\frac{32}{4} \times 25 = 200$

200 sts is a multiple of 8 sts, so cast on *200 sts*.

1 The width around the hem of the skirt and the stitch gauge of the yarn you are using determine the number of stitches you must cast on for the lower edge of the skirt. The number of stitches must be divisible by 8.

2 Cast on the required number of stitches.
1st row: (RS) *K7, P1, rep from * to end.
2nd row: K4, *P1, K7, rep from * to last 4 sts, P1, K3. Repeat these two rows for the required length, then bind off.

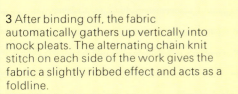

3 After binding off, the fabric automatically gathers up vertically into mock pleats. The alternating chain knit stitch on each side of the work gives the fabric a slightly ribbed effect and acts as a foldline.

4 It is easy to shape the fabric by decreasing two stitches in each pattern repeat: this is useful to avoid bulk around hips and waist. Simply knit two stitches together immediately before and after each "chain" knit stitch on the side of the fabric facing you. In the upper part of the sample shown above, there are five stitches, instead of seven, between the ribs.

5 This piece has been shaped by working two decrease rows so that there are finally only three stitches between ribs. It is possible to have wider pleats initially by casting on 2, 4, 6 or more stitches (depending on the width required) in addition to the 8 needed for each pattern repeat.

Fred Mancini

Making knife pleats

It is quite easy to adapt a skirt pattern, or to make up your own design, to include knife pleats. The width you need around the hem is important in calculating the cast-on stitches: it must be three times the waist measurement. The main fabric is knitted straight up from the hem with marker stitches to denote foldlines; the pleats may be knitted in position on the last row, although you can fold and sew them by hand if you prefer. To work the pleat row you need two extra double-pointed needles; these hold the stitches of the hidden folds under the pleat as you work stitches from all three needles together to anchor the pleats.

As there are a large number of stitches needed for a skirt with knife pleats, it is easiest to make it in two pieces with side seams. Or, use a circular needle to knit the skirt in rounds.

Waist measurement	24in
Width around hem	24in × 3 = 72in
Stitch gauge	26 sts = 4in
No. of sts around hem	$\frac{72}{4} \times 26 = 468$
No. of sts in each piece	$\frac{468}{2} = 234$

234 sts is a multiple of 12 sts
plus 6 extra (instead of 8),
so add 2 more sts and cast on *236 sts*.

1 Determine the width around the hem by multiplying the waist measurement by three. Work out the number of cast-on stitches according to the gauge and hem measurement. The stitches must be divisible by 12, plus 8 extra; if necessary, adjust the total by adding extra stitches.

2 Cast on required stitches using a pair of needles. **1st row** (RS) *K8, P1, K2, sl 1 purlwise, rep from * to last 8 sts, K8. **2nd row** *P11, K1, rep from * to last 8 sts, P8. Rep last 2 rows for required length, minus 1in (2.5cm) for waistband. The purl stitch marks the underlying fold of the pleat and the slip stitch the foldline.

3 Use the two double-pointed needles to "knit in" the pleats on the last (RS) row at the waist edge. Last row: K4, *sl next 4 sts onto first extra needle, sl next 4 sts onto second extra needle, then place first extra needle behind second one and hold both needles behind left-hand needle.

4 Continue with last row: (K tog 1 st from each of 3 needles) 4 times, rep from * to last 4 sts, K4. After drawing a loop through the 3 stitches being worked together, carefully drop the stitches from each of the needles individually.

5 The last row automatically pleats the fabric: the original purl stitches mark the underlying fold, while the slipped stitches make a distinctive foldline on the top edge of the fabric. Before pressing the fabric, baste the pleats, keeping them in straight vertical lines.

Making vertical pleats

Vertical pleats are worked sideways so that the cast-on and bound-off edges form the center back seam. To work out your own pleats, all you need to know are the waist measurement, length to hem and stitch gauge. From this information calculate the cast-on stitches, then follow these step-by-step instructions, knitting fabric to twice the waist measurement.

Working the fabric in two-color stripes makes an unusual variation of vertical pleats. When the pleats are folded the main color is on top and the underside of the fold is in a contrasting color. Carry the yarns loosely up one side (the waist edge) of the fabric when working stripes; these can later be hidden inside the waistband.

Length from waist to hem	20in
Stitch gauge	25 sts = 4in
No. of sts in main section	$\frac{20}{4} \times 25 = 125$
	(126, an even no.)
No. of sts in 1in hem	6

So total no. of cast-on sts is
126 + 6 or *132 sts*.

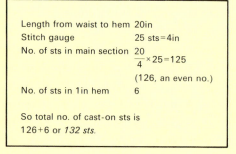

1 Work out the number of cast-on stitches according to the stitch gauge and length from waist to hem; allow 1in (2.5cm) extra for a turned-under hem. The stitches in the main section should be an even number.

2 Cast on the required stitches using a pair of needles. Beginning with a K row, work 13 rows stockinette st. **14th row** P across hem sts, *yo, P2 tog, rep from *to end. Work 5 more rows stockinette st. **20th row** P across hem sts, K tbl all sts to end. These 20 rows form the pattern.

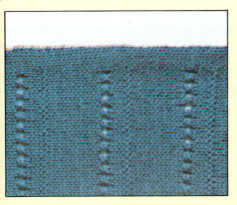

Fred Mancini

3 Continue in pattern until the fabric is twice the waist measurement, ending with a 20th row. Bind off. Join the cast-on and bound-off edges to form the center back seam. Notice that the hem is in plain stockinette stitch.

4 Turn the hem at the lower edge to the wrong side and slip stitch it in place. Baste the pleats in position at the waist edge: use the picot row to form the inner fold and the knit row to form the outer foldline. Also baste down the edge of the pleats for pressing.

5 Working the underside of the pleat in a different color looks most effective when the pleats are open. Simply work the first 14 pattern rows in one color (the main one) and then the next 6 rows in a contrasting color throughout. Here you can see the finished result.

Stitch Wise

Drop-stitch ribbing

Drop stitch patterns are not for beginners, but this one is fun to practice. Both sides of the fabric are interesting.
Cast on a multiple of 12 sts plus 1 extra.
1st row (RS) P3, *K1 tbl, P5 , rep from * ending with P3 instead of P5.
2nd row K2, *P3, K4, P1, K4, rep from * ending with K3.
3rd row *P3, K1 tbl, P3, K5, rep from * to last st, P1.
4th row K1, *P 5, K3, P1, K3, rep from * to end.
5th-7th rows Rep 3rd and 4th rows once more, then 3rd row again.
8th row K1, *P2, drop next st off needle and unravel 5 rows down, re-insert left-hand needle from front to back through st (with 5 strands behind) and K it catching

in strands—called drop 1 (D1), P2, K2, P3, K2, rep from * to end.
9th row P1, *K5, P3, K1 tbl, P3, rep from * to end.
10th row *K3, P1, K3, P5, rep from * to last st, K1.
11th-13th rows Rep 9th and 10th rows once more, then 9th row again.
14th row *K2, P3, K2, P2, D1, P2, rep from * to last st, K1.
Rep 3rd to 14th rows throughout.

Bubble-textured ribbing

Increase and decrease to form this fascinating texture of reverse stockinette stitch "bubbles" between knit ribs. The fabric is easy to knit, lies flat and requires no pressing.
Cast on a multiple of 8 sts plus 1 extra.

1st row (WS) P1, *K1, P1, K5, P1, rep from * to end.
2nd row K1, *P5, K1, P1, K1, rep from * to end.
3rd row P1, *pick up loop lying between needles and K tbl—called make 1 (M1), (K1, P1, K1) all into next st, M1, P1, P5 tog, P1, rep from * to end.
4th row K1, *P1, K1, P5, K1, rep from * to end.
5th row P1, *K5, P1, K1, P1, rep from * to end.
6th-8th rows Rep 4th and 5th rows once more, then 4th row again.
9th row P1, *P5 tog, P1, M1, (K1, P1, K1) all into next st, M1, P1, rep from * to end.
10th-12th rows Rep 2nd row, then 1st and 2nd rows again.
These 12 rows form the patt.

Girl's pleated skirt

Just the thing to complete your pretty skating outfit, this stockinette stitch skirt with picot edged pleats is a real eye-catcher.

Note This child's skirt can easily be adapted to fit an adult. Measure the waist and make the skirt width twice the waist measurement. The skirt length can be varied according to the number of stitches cast on.

Size
To fit, waist 20 in (51cm).
Length 12in (30cm) from waistband.

Gauge
20 sts and 32 rows to 4in (10cm) in patt on No. 6 (4mm) needles.

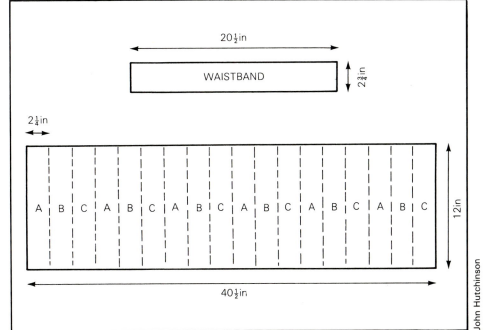

John Hutchinson

Materials
2oz (50g) of a sport weight 100% wool yarn in main color A
2oz (50g) each of 2 contrasting colors B and C
One pair No. 6 (4mm) knitting needles
22in (56cm) of 1¼ in (3cm)-wide elastic

To make
**Using No. 6 (4mm) needles and A, cast on 60 sts. Beg with a K row, work 13 rows in st st.
14th row P1, * yo, P2 tog, rep from * to last st, P1.
Beg with a K row, work 3 rows in st st.
18th row Using B, *K tbl, rep from * to end.
Using B, rep the first 17 patt rows.
Next row Using C, *K tbl, rep from * to end.'
Using C, rep first 17 patt rows.
Rep from ** 5 more times.
Bind off.

Waistband
Using No. 6 (4mm) needles and A, cast on 102 sts. Beg with a K row, work 21 rows in st st.
Bind off.

To finish
Pin and press the pleats into place. With the RS of skirt and waistband tog, sew the waistband to waist edge of skirt. Overlap ends of elastic and sew tog. Place elastic on WS of waistband, fold waistband in half over it and slipstitch down loosely. Join the center back seam and waistband seam. Fold the last two picot stitches up for the hem and slipstitch down.

Knitting / COURSE 49

*Expert knitting tips
*Suspended binding off
*Shaped binding off
*Selvages
*Stitch Wise: Mock Fair
 Isle patterns
*Pattern for a baby's sleeping
 bag and child's bathrobe

Expert knitting tips

If you are an enthusiastic knitter, you will be eager to expand your knowledge to include some of the special, practical techniques used by experts.

Two new methods of binding off are shown here. Suspended binding off is very useful if you have a tendency to work too tightly; it is a slightly looser version of a normal bind-off. Shaped binding off involves the "turning rows" technique to produce a sloping edge immediately before binding off in the usual way. It is an ideal way of producing neat shoulder shaping that is much easier to seam.

There are also some hints on working side selvages, whether for edges that are to be seamed or for an open fabric such as a scarf. Each selvage must be suitable for the fabric, as an edge that is too tight or loose distorts the fabric.

Suspended binding off

1 If you normally bind off too tightly, try this method. Knit the first two stitches in the usual way. Lift the first stitch over the second; don't let it drop off right-hand needle, keep it on left-hand needle point.

2 Take the right-hand needle in front of the stitch held on the left-hand needle and knit the next stitch on the left-hand needle in the usual way.

3 After knitting the stitch, slip both loops (the stitch just knitted and the held one) off the left-hand needle together.

4 Pull the edge gently with your right hand. You will see the first bound-off stitch "locking" in exactly the same way as a normal one.

5 There are now two stitches on right-hand needle: insert left-hand needle into the first of them and repeat suspended binding off process as far as necessary.

6 The final bound-off edge looks similar to a normal one except that the chain effect of the stitches is much looser due to "suspending" the binding off process.

Shaped binding off

1 At the right back shoulder edge, work to the (purl) row before the shoulder shaping begins. Purl to within the number of stitches quoted in the first bound-off group at the beginning of the next (knit) row—here it is 6 stitches.

2 Instead of purling to the end of the row, turn the work, so leaving the last 6 stitches unworked. Now slip the first stitch knitwise, then knit to the end of the row.

3 Purl to within the number of stitches in the second bound-off group. Here it is 6 stitches again: remember to leave the previous bound-off stitches unworked, making 12 unworked stitches in all.

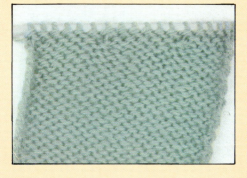

4 Turn the work, slip the first stitch and knit to the end of the row. Here the last group of knitted stitches represents the final number of bound-off stitches; if this is not the case, continue purling and turning until all the groups of bound-off stitches have been accounted for.

5 On the following row, purl across all the stitches even though the fabric is gaping slightly where the work has been turned and the stitches at the left-hand edge have remained unworked for several rows.

6 The finished bound-off edge slopes down from the left to the right without the "stepped" effect of a more usual shoulder edge. On the left back shoulder edge, reverse the work by starting the shaping on a knit row.

Selvages

1 Side edges of knitting must have a neat, firm edge for seaming. To make a selvage when you are working in stockinette stitch, slip the first stitch purlwise on every row and always knit the last stitch in every row.

2 To make a side selvage when working in garter stitch, bring the yarn to the front of the work at the beginning of every row and slip the first stitch purlwise. Take the yarn to the back between the needles and knit to the end of the row.

3 Sometimes both edges of knitting will show—when knitting a scarf for example —and must therefore be neat. In garter stitch, simply slip the first stitch in every row. When working in stockinette stitch, slip the first and last stitch knitwise in every row to form a chain effect. Work the purl rows in the usual way.

Fred Mancini

45

Stitch Wise

Mock Fair Isle patterns

True Fair Isle patterns do not use more than two colors in any one row of knitting, although any number of colors may be used throughout the design as a whole. Mock Fair Isle employs a solid-colored yarn for the background and a variegated one (either in a selection of different colors or in tones of one color) to create striking, multi-colored patterns which sometimes resemble true Fair Isle.

Try to choose a solid color to coordinate with, rather than blend with or match, the variegated yarn: otherwise the colors may become too subtle and the pattern will lose its distinction.

The fabric samples here show variations on the mock Fair Isle theme with solid backgrounds and variegated patterns, as well as variegated backgrounds with solid-colored patterns.

These designs are worked from conventional charts using traditional Fair Isle patterns and motifs. The two balls of yarn are used in the pattern rows with the color not in use being carried across the back of the work.

Repeat 16 sts
and 16 rows

Repeat 25 sts

Baby's sleeping bag and child's bathrobe

Knit this cozy twosome with bands of Mock Fair Isle in variegated yarns.

Sizes
To fit 18-20[20-22]in (46-51[51-56]cm) chest. Length, 21¾[26]in (56[66]cm). Sleeve seam, 7[9]in (18[23]cm).
Note Directions for the larger size are in brackets []; if there is only one set of figures it applies to both sizes.

Materials
Bathrobe
6[10]oz (160[260]g) of a knitting worsted in main shade (A)
2[3]oz (40[60]g) in contrasting color (B)
Sleeping bag
Same as bathrobe, plus 1oz (20g) (A)
1 pair each Nos. 2 and 4 (3 and 3¾mm) knitting needles
20[24]in (50[60]cm) zipper (open-ended for bathrobe)

Gauge
24 sts and 32 rows to 4in (10cm) in stockinette st on No. 4 (3¾mm) needles.

Back and fronts
Using No. 4 (3¾mm) needles and A, cast on 145[173] sts.

End st · End · Rep 28 sts · Start · Start main
2nd size sleeve · patt and 1st
size sleeve

□ = main   x = contrasting

Rod Delroy

1st row K3, *P1, K1, rep from * to last 2 sts, K2.

2nd row K2, *P1, K1, rep from * to last st, K1.

Rep last 2 rows once more.

Next row K to end.

Next row K2, P to last 2 sts, K2.

Rep last 2 rows until work measures $1\frac{1}{2}[2\frac{1}{4}]$in (4[6]cm); end with a WS row. Keeping 2 sts at each end in garter st in A throughout, cont in patt from chart until 59 rows have been completed. Cont in A only, work 3 rows; end with a WS row.

Next row K14[17], *K2 tog, K27[21], rep from * 3[5] times more, K2 tog, K to end. 140[166] sts.

Still keeping 2 sts in garter st at each end, cont straight for $4[4\frac{3}{4}]$in (10[12]cm); end with a WS row.

Next row K13[16], *K2 tog, K26[20], rep form * 3[5] times more, K2 tog, K to end. 135[159] sts.

Cont straight until work measures 17[20]in (44[51]cm) or length required; end with a WS row.

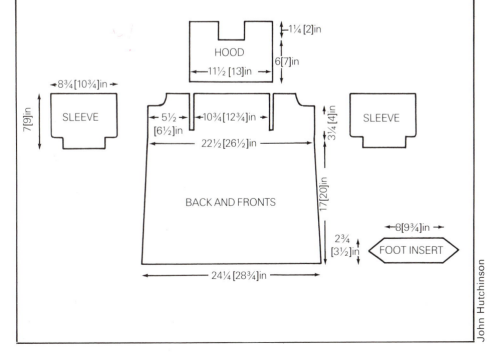

John Hutchinson

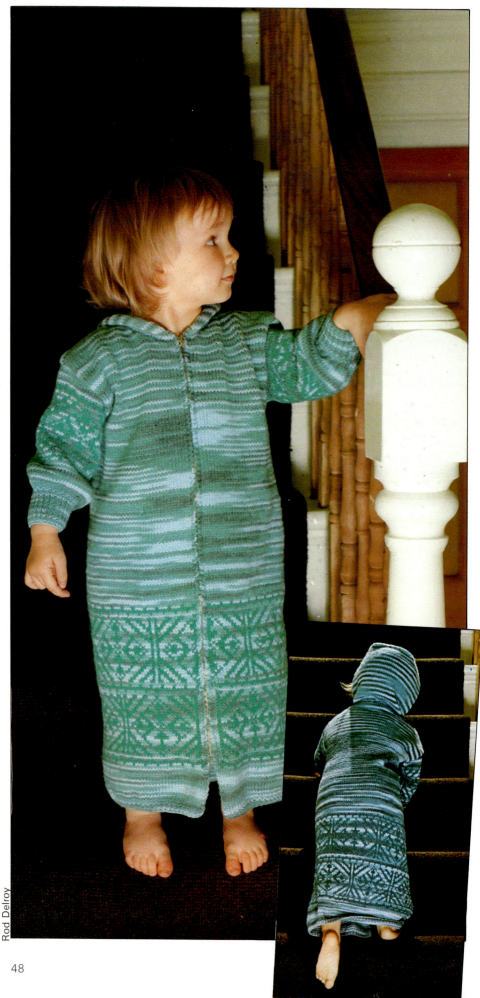

Divide for armholes

Next row K33[39], bind off 2, K64[76], bind off 2, K to end.
Cont on last 33[39] sts for left front until armhole measures $3\frac{1}{4}$[4]in (8[10]cm); end with a RS row.

Shape neck

Bind off 6 sts at beg of next row, 2 sts at beg of foll 2 alternate rows, then dec one st at beg of foll 3[5] alternate rows. Cont on rem 20[24] sts until armhole measures $4\frac{3}{4}$[6]in (12[15]cm); end with a P row. Bind off. With WS of work facing, rejoin yarn to rem 65[77] sts for back. Cont straight until armholes measure same as front; end with a P row. Bind off. With WS of work facing, rejoin yarn to 33[39] sts for right front and cont to match left front, reversing shaping.

Sleeves

Using No. 2 (3mm) needles and A, cast on 35[43] sts.
1st row K1, *P1, K1, rep from * to end.
2nd row P1, *K1, P1, rep from * to end.
Rep last 2 rows for $1\frac{1}{2}$[2]in (4[5]cm); end with a 2nd row. Change to No. 4 ($3\frac{3}{4}$mm) needles.
Next row K twice into first st, *K1, K twice into next st, rep from * to end. 57[71]sts.
Beg with a P row, cont in stockinette st until work measures $2\frac{1}{4}$[4]in (6[10]cm); end with a P row, inc 4 sts evenly on last row. Work first 31 rows of patt, beg and ending rows foll chart. Cont in A only until sleeve measures 7[9]in (18[23]cm); end with a P row. Bind off.

Hood

Using No. 4 ($3\frac{3}{4}$mm) needles and A, cast on 69[78] sts. Keeping 2 sts at each end in garter st, cont in stockinette st until work measures 6[7]in (15[18]cm); end with a WS row.
Next row K26[29], bind off 17[20], K to end.
Cont on last 26[39] sts for $1\frac{1}{4}$[2]in (3[5]cm); end with a WS row. Break off yarn and leave sts on a thread. With WS of work facing, rejoin yarn to rem 26[29] sts and work to match first side.

Foot insert (sleeping bag only)

Using No. 4[$3\frac{3}{4}$mm] needles and A, cast on 48[58] sts. P 1 row. Cont in stockinette st, inc one st at each end of every row until there are 72[86] sts; end with a P row. Dec one st at each end of next and every foll row until 48[58] sts rem. Bind off.

To finish

Press or block, according to yarn used. Join shoulder and sleeve seams. Sew in sleeves. Graft seam at top of hood, then sew side edges of this piece to bound-off sts. Sew on hood around neck edge. Sew in zipper and foot insert if required. Press seams.

Knitting / COURSE 50

Remodeling knitted garments

There are a number of different alterations you can make to a finished knitted garment. The most frequently-made alterations include adjusting the length (maybe to fit a growing child), re-styling an out-of-date garment and livening up a classic. The garments shown on page 52 illustrate some ways of making these kinds of alterations; a classic sweater becomes a fashionable shirt when it is lengthened (by adding more knitting onto the main fabric) and extra

trimmings, such as a collar, tie, pocket top and handkerchief, are added.
It is worthwhile buying extra yarn in the same dye lot for this purpose, especially if you are making a child's garment which you will probably need to repair or enlarge. Otherwise the best method of lengthening a garment is usually by adding contrasting stripes, as on the sweater on page 52.
Many alterations involve unpicking the garment's seams. Seaming stitches are

often difficult to see in knitted fabric; anticipate and overcome this when finishing the garment by running a length of fine thread in a contrasting color under the stitches as you sew—this indicates the position of stitches for unpicking later. There are two important things to remember when altering knitting—demonstrated in the step-by-step sequences shown in this Knitting course. First, NEVER cut the fabric and second, there is no need to waste unraveled yarn that can be recycled.

Altering the length of a piece of knitting

To lengthen or shorten a knitted fabric, never cut the fabric itself. Cutting is an extremely difficult process and should only be undertaken by experts in special circumstances. Instead of cutting, unpick the seams and divide the fabric as shown

in the step-by-step photographs.
First, examine the garment to find the best position for altering the length: a sweater with short or long body and sleeves needs extra length added or subtracted two or three rows above the waistband or cuff.

If you are lengthening the sweater, note the exact number of rows below the adjustment point (including those in the waistband); you must knit these exactly as before after adding the extra length to the main section.

Lengthening

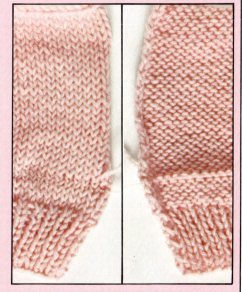

Fred Mancini

1 Unpick any seams—such as side or sleeve seams—to about 2in (5cm) above the adjustment point (here it is marked with a line of pins) to give you freedom to manipulate the needles when you re-knit.

2 Insert the point of a knitting needle into the head of a stitch in the adjustment row—one or two stitches in from the right-hand edge of the fabric as shown.

3 Loosen the stitch with the needle, then use your thumb and forefinger to pull the stitch. As you draw the stitch into a long, loose loop the other stitches in the row will tighten across the width of the fabric; this is most evident on the back, where the row becomes a hard, horizontal ridge.
continued

4 Cut the long loop. Gently pull the fabric apart at the right-hand edge until the loops of two or three stitches become loose.

5 Use the point of a knitting needle to draw one cut end of yarn through each stitch separately to unravel the stitches.

6 Continue to pull the fabric apart gently and unravel the cut end of yarn until you expose two sets of stitches. At the end of the row the fabric should be split into two pieces.

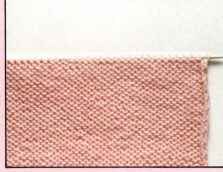

7 To add extra length you must pick up the stitches at the lower edge of the main piece. With the wrong side of the work facing, start at the left-hand edge and insert the knitting needle from front to back through the first stitch.

8 Continue picking up the stitches in this way until they are all on the needle. The wrong side of the work is facing for the next (purl) row.

9 Join on the yarn in the usual way and continue in stockinette stitch for the length you need, then work any ribbing. Here four rows have been worked past the division. Although you are knitting downward, the new stitches lie in the same direction as before so that the joining is undetectable.

Shortening

1 Divide the fabric as described in steps 1 to 3 of "lengthening" but split it in two places, with the section between the divisions measuring the same distance as the garment must be taken up.

2 Remove the unwanted section, leaving the two sets of loops exposed—those at the lower edge of the main section and those just above any ribbed section or hem.

3 Join the remaining two sections by grafting the stitches together as shown in Volume 8, page 41. Grafting also produces an invisible joining.

Recycling yarn

There is no need to discard old, unraveled yarn, especially if you are altering a garment to give it a new lease on life. The shirt-style sweater on page 52 uses unwound yarn from the lower edge of the classic version in the stripes; this is an economical and sensible use of old yarn, since it is virtually impossible to obtain yarn in the same dye lot later. Yarn that has been knitted even for a short time is crinkled and must be steamed smooth before re-use. Any yarn that you want to re-use must be in good condition—if the fabric has felted, it will be difficult to unravel the stitches. You will probably be restricted to re-using fairly plain yarns such as knitting-worsted—many fashion yarns are too textured or hairy to unwind successfully.

1 As you unravel the yarn you must rewind it straight onto a frame: a wire coat hanger bent into the shape shown above is suitable for this purpose.

2 Unless you are dividing the knitting to shorten a section, unpick the garment so that it is in sections. Beginning at a bound-off edge, rewind the yarn into a skein around the wire frame. The unpicked yarn will be crinkly.

3 Don't wind the yarn too thickly around the frame or the steam will have difficulty in penetrating completely. Steam the folds of yarn thoroughly by holding them above a pan of boiling water or a kettle. Keep your hand away from the steam.

4 Leave the wet yarn wound around the frame until it is completely dry—hang it outdoors on a warm, windy day (but not in sunlight) or indoors away from direct heat.

5 As it dries and the moisture evaporates, the yarn becomes taut and the crinkles disappear. Before knitting with the yarn again, wind it loosely into balls.

Fred Mancini

Classic shirt-style sweaters

Here is a classic sweater which, if you get tired of it, can be updated by lengthening the body and sleeves and adding fashionable details like the collar, tie, pocket top and hankie. The directions are easily adapted for updating any simple sweater you have already knitted.

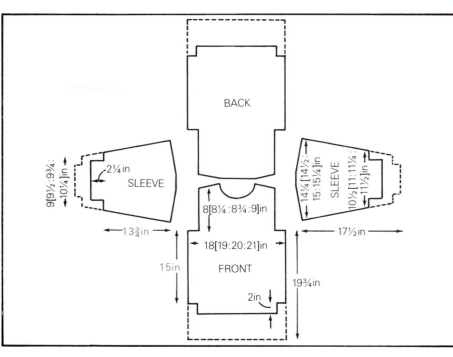

Sizes
To fit 32[34:36:38]in (83[87:92:97]cm) bust.
Classic sweater length, 23[23¼:23¾:24]in (58[59:60:61]cm).
Sleeve seam, 13¾in (35cm).
Shirt-style sweater length, 27¾[28:28½:28¾]in (70[71:72:73]cm).
Sleeve seam, 17½in (45cm).
Note: Directions for the larger sizes are in brackets []; if there is only one set of figures it applies to all sizes.

Materials
  Classic sweater *15[15:16:17]oz (400[400:425:450]g) of a sport yarn in main shade (A)*
  Shirt-style sweater *2[2:3:3]oz (50[50:75:75]g) in contrasting color (B) for lengthening*
  4[4:5:5]oz (100[100:125:125]g) in contrasting color (C)
  1 pair each Nos. 3 and 5 (3¼ and 4mm) knitting needles

Gauge
22 sts and 30 rows to 4in (10cm) in stockinette st on No. 5 (4mm) needles.

Classic sweater

Back
Using No. 3 (3¼mm) needles and A, cast on 98[104:110:114] sts. Work 2in (5cm) K1, P1 ribbing. Change to No. 5 (4mm) needles. Beg with a K row, cont in stockinette st until work measures 15in (38cm); end with a P row.

Shape armholes
Bind off 10[11:12:12] sts at beg of next 2 rows. Cont straight until work measures 23[23¼:23¾:24]in (58[59:60:61]cm); end with a P row.

Shape shoulders
Bind off 7 sts at beg of next 4 rows and

8[9:10:11] sts at beg of foll 2 rows. Leave rem 34[36:38:40] sts on a spare needle.

Front
Work as for back until front measures 20½[20¾:21¼:21¾]in (52[53:54:55]cm); end with a P row.

Shape neck
Next row K29[30:31:32] sts, turn and leave rem sts on a spare needle.
Dec one st at neck edge on next 7 rows. Cont straight until front measures same as back to shoulder; end at armhole edge.

Shape shoulder
Bind off 7 sts at beg of next and foll alternate row. Work 1 row. Bind off rem 8[9:10:11] sts. With RS facing, sl center 20[22:24:26] sts onto a holder, rejoin yarn to next st and K to end. Finish to match first side.

Sleeves
Using No. 3 (3¼mm) needles and A, cast on 58[60:62:64] sts. Work 20 rows K1, P1 ribbing. Change to No. 5 (4mm) needles. Beg with a K row, cont in stockinette st, inc one st at each end of 7th and every foll 8th row until there are 78[80:82:84] sts. Cont straight until sleeve measures 13¾ (35cm); end with a P row. Mark each end of last row. Work a further 1⅛in (3cm) stockinette st; end with a P row.

Shape top
Bind off 7 sts at beg of next 10 rows. Bind off rem 8[10:12:14] sts.

Neckband
Join right shoulder seam. Using No. 3 (3¼mm) needles, A and with RS facing, pick up and K 14 sts down left front neck, K across 20[22:24:26] sts at center front, pick up and K 14 sts up right front neck and K across 34[36:38:40] back sts. 82[86:90:94] sts. Work 7 rows K1, P1 ribbing. Bind off loosely in ribbing.

To finish
Press or block, according to yarn used. Join left shoulder and neckband seam. Set in sleeves, sewing 1⅛in (3cm) above markers to bound-off sts at underarm. Join side and sleeve seams. Press seams.

Shirt-style sweater
To make back and front of classic sweater 4¾in (12cm) longer, pull thread above ribbing and put main sts onto a No. 5 (4mm) needle to knit downward.
Next row Using C, K to end.
Next row Using C, K4, P to last 4 sts, K4. Rep these 2 rows 23 times more, working in stripe sequence of 4 rows C, 6 rows each of A and C, 12 rows B, and 6 rows each of C, A and C. Change to No. 3 (3¼mm) needles and A. K1 row.
Next row K4, *K1, P1, rep from * to last 4 sts, K4.
Rep last row 4 times more. Bind off.

To make sleeves of classic sweater 2¾in (7cm) longer, pull thread above and put main sts onto a No. 5 (4mm) needle to knit downward. Cont in stockinette st and stripe sequence of 6 rows each of C, A, B, A, C, **at same time** dec one st at each end of 3rd and three full 8th rows. 50[52:54:56] sts. Change to No. 3 (3¼mm) needles and A. Work 12 rows K1, P1 ribbing. Bind off.

Collar
Using No. 3 (3¼mm) needles and B, cast on 22[26:30:34] sts. Work 2 rows K1, P1 ribbing. Cont to rib, casting on 6 sts at beg of next 14 rows. 106[110:114:118] sts. Rib 24 more rows. Bind off in ribbing.

Tie
Using No. 3 (3¼mm) needles and C, cast on 3 sts.
Next row K1, P1, K1.
Next row Inc in first st, rib to end.
Next row Rib to last 2 sts, inc in next st, rib 1.
Rep last 2 rows until there are 13 sts. Cont straight until tie measures 47in (120cm). Bind off.

Pocket top
Using No. 3 (3¼mm) needles and B, cast on 22 sts. Work 8 rows K1, P1 ribbing. Bind off in ribbing.

Hankie (make 2 pieces)
Using No. 3 (3¼mm) needles and C, cast on 16 sts. Work 8 rows K1, P1 ribbing. Dec one st at each end of next and foll alternate rows until 2 sts rem. K2 tog. Fasten off.

To finish
Rejoin seams, leaving striped section on back and front open for side slits. Unpick original neckband. Be careful to bind off front and back neck sts. Sew collar in position around neck edge. Position pocket top and hankie as desired and sew in place.

*Front flap with button fastening
*Tailored pants pockets
*Pedal pushers: adapting the pattern; directions for making

Front flap with button fastening

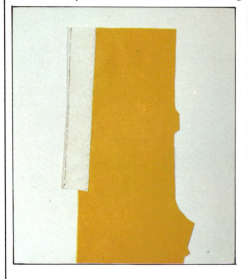

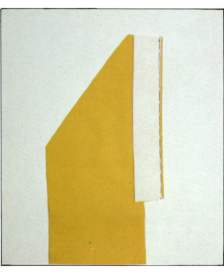

1 Baste interfacing to wrong side of pants fronts and catch-stitch interfacing to foldline of placket facing. To finish outer edge of facing, overcast it together with the interfacing or zig-zag stitch.

2 Baste interfacing to wrong side of side front placket facings. With right sides together, baste and stitch placket facings to side fronts making $\frac{1}{4}$in (6mm) seams.

3 Press seams open. Finish placket facings by overcasting or zig-zag stitching together with interfacing.

4 Turn placket facings to wrong side and press well. Staystitch the angle at lower end. Baste across the top to secure.

5 With right sides together, baste and stitch the front and side front pants pieces together to the bottom of the opening. Stitch the placket facings together across lower edges. Do not stitch through pants front.

6 On the inside, clip the side front seam allowance only, almost to the stay-stitching at the bottom of the opening. Press the seam open.

7 On the right side, sew a bar tack at the bottom of the opening to reinforce this point (see Volume 2, page 63). Before completing front fastening, stitch seams and finish pockets.

8 Baste the interfacing to wrong side of waistbands and catch-stitch it to foldline. With right sides together, baste long waistband to pants back and side fronts, overlapping ends $\frac{5}{8}$in (1.5cm) more than placket facings. Baste short waistband to front flap, overlapping ends $\frac{5}{8}$in (1.5cm). Sew both waistbands in place. Grade interfacing and seam allowances.

9 With right sides together, fold waistbands along foldlines and stitch across ends. Trim interfacing and cut across corners. Turn waistbands right side out and baste folded edge. On the inside, turn under seam allowance and hem in place. Press. Complete front fastenings.

Tailored pants pockets

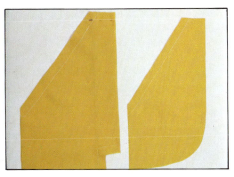

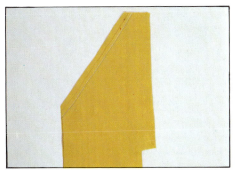

1 Staystitch along the pocket position on the pants side front, the pocket facing and the lower edge of placket facing to prevent stretching.

2 With right sides together, baste and stitch the pocket facing to the side front. Grade the seam allowances.

3 Turn the pocket facing away from the pants and press the seam allowance toward the facing. Understitch the seam allowances to the facing.

4 Turn the facing to the inside and topstitch along the sewn edge, stitching $\frac{1}{4}$in (6mm) in from edge. Press.

5 On the wrong side, lay the pocket section over the pocket facing with the wrong side of the pocket on top. Matching waist and side edges, baste and stitch around pocket outer edges through pocket thicknesses only.

6 To finish the outer edge of pocket overcast or zig-zag stitch the seam allowances together. Press from right side using press cloth as directed in Volume 10, page 78.

Mike Berend

55

Pedal pushers

Party time or vacation time—team up these pants with the middy blouse in Volume 10, page 78, choosing your fabric to suit the occasion.

Stuart Macleod

Adapting the pattern

The pedal pushers are made by adapting the pattern for the basic pants from the Stitch by Stitch Pattern Pack, available in sizes 10-20, which correspond to sizes 8-18 in ready-made clothes.

Materials
*3 sheets of tracing paper 36×40in
    (approx 90×100cm)
Flexible curve, yardstick*

1 Trace the pants front and back pattern pieces, marking the grain lines and lengthening and shortening lines.
2 On the front and back tracings, measure up from the lower edge 15¾in (40cm) and draw a horizontal line across the pattern pieces . This will be the finished length.

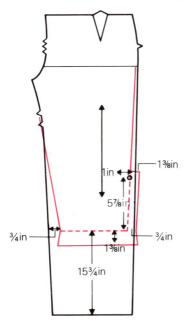

3 To make the leg slightly narrower, measure in from the inside and outside leg cutting lines ¾in (2cm) and mark. From the mark at the outside leg, draw the new cutting line from the hemline, tapering into the original cutting line at the hip. At the inside leg, draw the new cutting line from the mark at the hemline, tapering into the original cutting line at the bottom notch.
4 Mark length of the slit at side seamline 6in (15cm) up from lower edge. Before cutting the pattern along these new lines, add a 1⅜in (3.5cm) hem allowance and side facing, measuring from side seamline and hemline, and extending facing 1in (2.5cm) above slit.
5 To shape the side edges of the hem allowance, turn the hem allowance up and cut along these edges, following the inside and outside leg cutting lines.
6 To mark the new seamline through the center of the pattern, measure across the hemline and mark the center (do not include the facing allowance). Measure

along the lengthening and shortening line and mark the center. Using a yard-stick, draw the center line from hem cutting line to waistline. The dart is omitted but half the dart allowance is taken from the side edge and the other half is allowed for in button adjustment.

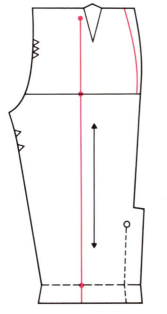

7 Measure the dart allowance at the top edge and halve this measurement. Measure this amount in from the side cutting lines at the waist edge. Using a flexible curve, redraw the side seam curve from this new waist edge.
8 Before separating the front along the center line, the pocket position is marked at the side, and the pocket pattern made. For the pocket position, measure down side seam from waist seam 6½in (16.5cm) and mark. Draw pocket line from mark to center of waist seamline.

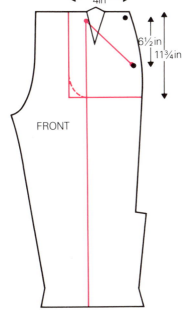

9 For the pocket facing and pocket section, the shape of the pocket is drawn

onto the pattern and then traced. To do this, measure in along the waist cutting line 4in (10cm) and mark. Then measure down the side cutting line 11¾in (30cm) and mark. From the marks at waist and side, draw two lines at right angles to form the pocket corner. Using a flexible curve, reshape the corner as shown. Trace pocket shape.

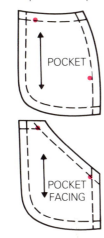

10 On the new pocket pattern, add a ⅝in (1.5cm) seam allowance to the curved edge. Mark the grain line. Trace the pocket facing and add ⅝in (1.5cm) seam allowance to the curved edge and the slanted edge. Mark the grain line.

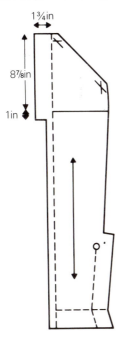

11 Cut the front pants pattern along center line to separate pattern, adding ⅝in (1.5cm) seam allowances to both edges. For placket facing, measure down center line of side front pattern 8⅞in (22.5cm) from waist cutting line and mark. Add facing to edge of opening, making it 1⅜in (4.5cm) wide from original cutting line, and 1in (2.5cm) longer than opening. Repeat with pattern for pants front section. The center line will now

Brian Mayor

57

be the foldline for facing and the front leg seamline. On the side fronts, cut along pocket line and add $\frac{5}{8}$in (1.5cm) seam allowance to this edge.

parallel with the grain line, draw the center line from this mark to the waistline. Take half the dart allowance from the side edge as directed for the front. The other half is taken from the center seam.

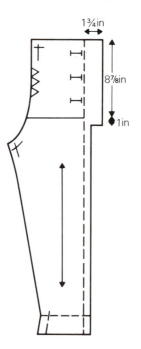

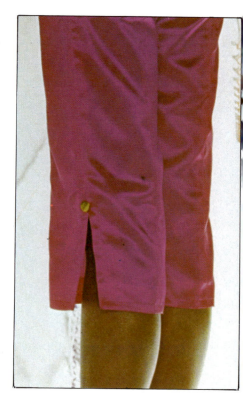

12 Mark the three buttonhole positions on the front $\frac{5}{8}$in (1.5cm) in from placket foldline, the first being $2\frac{3}{8}$in (6cm) below waist cutting line and the other two at $2\frac{3}{8}$in (6cm) intervals. Each buttonhole is $\frac{3}{4}$in (2cm) long. Mark the grain line on both pieces parallel to center seam.

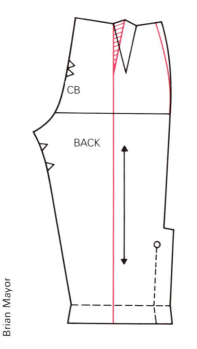

Brian Mayor

13 Mark the center of the pants back leg at the hem cutting line (do not include facing allowance). Keeping the line

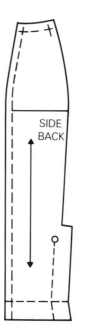

14 Draw a line from the center line to the center top of the dart. Start the line from the same level as the dart point and finish at the waist cutting line. Cut along the center line and separate the pattern. The shaded section in the diagram at left is cut away and a $\frac{5}{8}$in (1.5cm) seam allowance added to both edges.

FRONT WAISTBAND

		CF		

15 Two waistbands are needed, one for the flap and one for the back and side fronts. For the front flap waistband, measure across the pattern between the placket foldline and the center front. Double this amount and add an extra $1\frac{1}{4}$in (3cm) for seam allowances. Make the waistband $3\frac{1}{2}$in (9cm) wide to give a finished width of $1\frac{1}{8}$in (3cm). Seam allowances of $\frac{5}{8}$in (1.5cm) have been included on each edge. Mark the foldline along the center of waistband.

PANTS WAISTBAND

		CB			

16 For the long waistband, measure the waist from the center back seam to side seam and from side seam to the edge of the placket facing. Double this amount. Add $\frac{3}{4}$in (2cm) seam allowance; seams are $\frac{5}{8}$in (1.5cm) at each end but $\frac{3}{8}$in (1cm) is subtracted to allow for placket facing seams. It should be same width as front waistband. Mark foldline.

17 To make placket facing pattern for side fronts, measure a rectangle onto tracing or pattern paper $1\frac{3}{4} \times 10$in (4.5 × 25cm). Cut out pattern. Seam allowances have already been included.

Directions for making

Suggested fabrics
Cotton or synthetic sailcloth, poplin, gabardine, linen and linen-finish fabric.

Materials
36in (90cm)- and 45in (115cm)-
  wide fabric with or without nap:
  For all sizes: $2\frac{5}{8}$yd (2.4m)
54in (140cm)-wide fabric with or
  without nap:
  Sizes 10, 12: $2\frac{1}{8}$yd (1.8m)
  Sizes 14, 16: $2\frac{1}{8}$yd (1.9m)
  Sizes 18, 20: $2\frac{1}{4}$yd (2m)
36in (90cm)-wide interfacing:
  For all sizes: $\frac{3}{8}$yd (.3m)
Matching thread
Ten $\frac{3}{4}$in (2cm)-diameter buttons
2 pants hooks and eyes

Key to adjusted pattern pieces
A Pants front   Cut 2
B Pants side front   Cut 2
C Pants back   Cut 2
D Pants side back   Cut 2
E Pocket   Cut 2
F Pocket facing   Cut 2
G Front waistband   Cut 1
H Pants waistband   Cut 1
I Placket facing   Cut 2
Interfacing: use piece I   Cut 4
    use piece G   Cut 1
    use piece H   Cut 1

1 Prepare the fabric and cut out. Transfer all pattern markings to fabric before removing pattern.

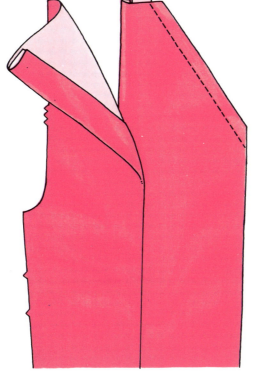

2 Staystitch pocket seamline on side fronts and the bottom of the opening on

fronts and side fronts after applying interfacing and facing to plackets (see page 54). Stitch front leg seams and front openings on each front (see page 54). Sew bar tack across bottom of placket.

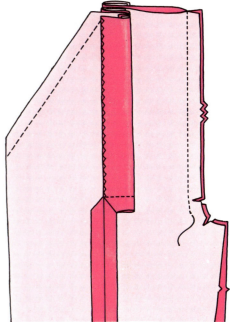

3 With right sides together, baste and stitch the front crotch seam to within $1\frac{1}{4}$in (3.5cm) of inside leg seam. Clip curve and press seam open.

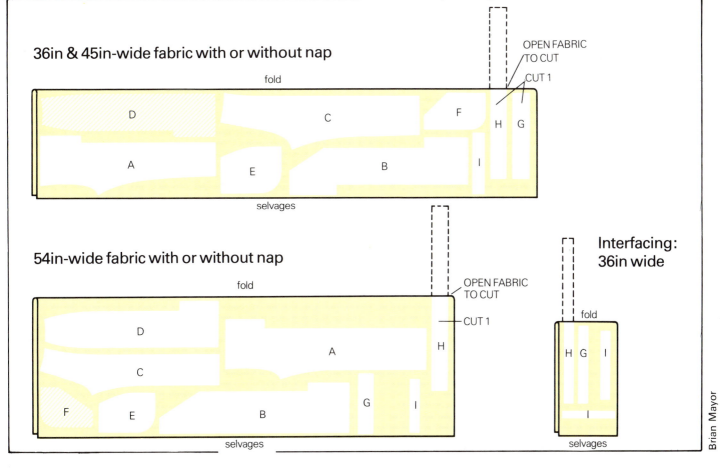

36in & 45in-wide fabric with or without nap

54in-wide fabric with or without nap

Interfacing: 36in wide

Brian Mayor

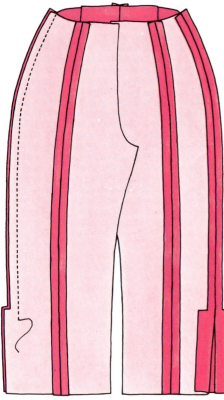

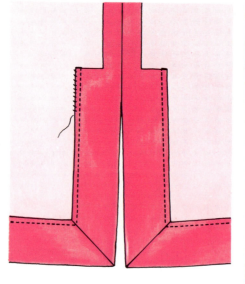

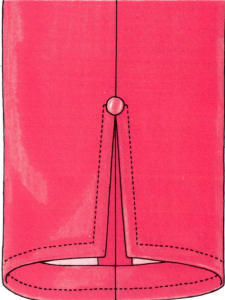

6 Complete waistline by attaching waistband to pants as shown on page 55. Make buttonholes and try on the pants to find the button positions. Sew on buttons and hooks and eyes to fasten placket openings. Turn up hem and finish slit facing as shown in Volume 10, page 57.

7 When hem is complete, topstitch around the hem and the slit opening, $\frac{1}{4}$in (6mm) in from the edge. A button may be added to the top of the opening for a decorative finish.

4 Make pants pockets as directed on page 55. With right sides together, baste and stitch the back leg seams. Press seams open.

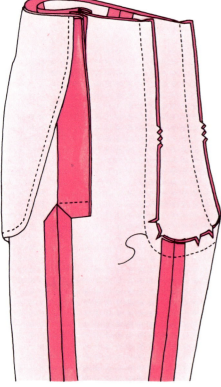

5 With right sides together, slip one leg inside the other. Matching notches and inside leg seams, baste and stitch the crotch seam. Clip curve and press seam open.

Stuart Macleod

*Handling and sewing tips
 for bias-cut fabrics
*Leveling a bias-cut hem
*Tailor-bound hem
*Pattern for a bias-cut
 evening dress

Handling and sewing tips for bias-cut fabrics

A true bias is formed diagonally when one selvage is folded at right angles across the warp of the fabric and parallel to the weft. The true bias of the fabric therefore runs at an angle of 45° to the straight grain.

When working with bias-cut fabric, try to handle it as little as possible during the construction of the garment, since it has a tendency to stretch.

In preparing the fabric for cutting, lay it out unfolded on a flat surface so that any double pieces can be cut individually. If this is not possible, try to avoid stretching or pulling the fold of the fabric during cutting.

Pin all the pieces in place before cutting out, with the exception of the facings, which may have to be adjusted and cut out at a later stage—often on the straight grain to give additional support to the bias edge.

Check carefully that patterns match, moving double pieces as necessary. It is best to avoid fabrics with a nap, pile, one-way pattern, or diagonal weave (such as gabardine) unless you are a very experienced dressmaker. Plaids and stripes can be used to advantage and some interesting design effects achieved.

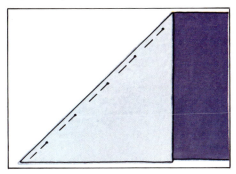

1 To find the true bias for cutting bias strips—useful for binding edges, as in the tailor-bound hem on page 62, and for making tube straps, as on the dress on page 63—fold the fabric so that the warp threads are at right angles to the weft threads. Pin about $1\frac{1}{4}$in (3cm) away from the folded edge all along length. Cut through fold and mark off strips parallel to the cut edge.

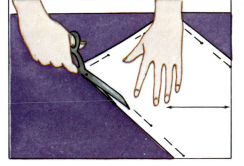

2 When cutting out, lay the pattern on the fabric with the grain line parallel to the selvage. Use sharp scissors and keep the fabric as flat as possible with one hand while cutting. Keep the pieces flat after cutting to avoid pulling them out of shape, and use short, firm, basting stitches when fitting.

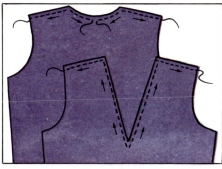

3 Staystitching is essential and should be done from the wide to the narrow edge of the pattern piece. If the direction of the grain changes—on necklines and collars, for example—stitch from one edge to the center, then from the other direction to the center.

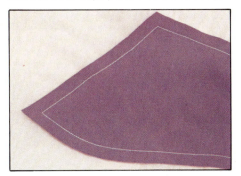

4 To help prevent bias-cut fabrics from slipping or pulling out of shape during construction, baste each piece to tissue paper before making garment. Remove tissue paper by pulling away gently after the main seams are stitched.

5 Stay tape can be used to reinforce shaped or weak edges. Normally, it is used instead of staystitching, in conjunction with a facing to which it is applied, centered on the seamline, after the facing is basted in place.

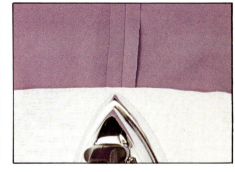

6 Press bias-cut seams carefully after each stage in the garment's construction, but do not run the iron along a bias-cut seam as this will pull and stretch the fabric. Press with a press cloth as shown in Volume 10, page 78.

Mike Berend

Leveling a bias-cut hem

The hemline on a bias-cut garment will probably droop a lot in places, as the uneven weight tends to distort the fabric after it has been hung for a few days. To straighten the hem and make sure that it is level before hemming, enlist the help of a friend. Try on the garment, wearing the shoes and underclothes you intend to wear. If it is a dress hem, stand on a low table or chair, since this makes it easier for the fitter to see the hem and make adjustments.

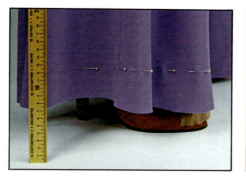

1 Decide on the length and, using a hem marker or ruler, mark the same measurement up from floor level, about every 2in (5cm) all around. Pin and baste. This will be the hemline.

2 Mark the hem allowance and trim away excess fabric. Baste the hem in place and try on the garment again to make sure it is level. Adjust if necessary. Remove and complete hem.

A tailor-bound hem

A tailor-bound hem is a very neat way of turning up a hem and enclosing the raw edge. The binding makes only one hem fold necessary. It can be made from the main garment fabric or lining fabric. Or you can use purchased bias binding. It is a particularly useful method when making a garment from a thick fabric such as tweed, or where extra fullness makes the hem bulky, such as on a very flared skirt.

1 After adjusting the hem to the correct height and marking the hemline with basting, you must reduce any fullness in the hem before the hem can be sewn in place. On wide-paneled garments, such as the dress right, gathering will be essential. Use a long machine stitch, working about $\frac{1}{4}$in (6mm) from raw edge; pull up bobbin thread until hem fits. Do not gather too tightly.

2 Cut enough bias strips approximately 1in (2.5cm) wide to fit the hem plus seam allowances, or use ready-made bias binding. After joining them to make one long strip, press in half along the length. Fold under $\frac{1}{4}$in (6mm) along one edge and press again.

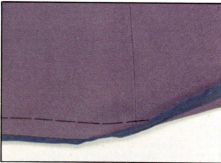

3 Matching the raw edge you have just folded to the raw hem edge, and with right sides together, baste and stitch along the $\frac{1}{4}$in (6mm) foldline. Press the binding away from the hemline.

4 Fold the binding over the hem edge to enclose all raw edges, but do not fold under the other binding edge as in ordinary bias binding. Baste and stitch through binding and hem only, following the seamline of the binding. Press.

5 Baste the hem to the garment close to the lower edge of the binding and catch-stitch or invisibly hand-hem the bound edge to the garment. The stitching will be invisible from both sides. Remove all basting and press the hemline only.

Bias-cut
evening dress

Simple, classic lines and careful cutting make this evening dress something very special. Directions for the matching bolero are given in the next course on page 70.

Adapting the pattern

Measurements

The dress is made by adapting the pattern for the basic dress taken from the Stitch by Stitch Pattern Pack, available in sizes 10-20, which correspond to sizes 8-18 in ready-made clothes. The pattern adjustment on the length of the dress applies to all sizes. To alter this length adjust by lengthening or shortening the hemline and alter fabric yardage.

Materials

4 sheets of tracing paper 60×36in (approx. 150×90cm)
Yardstick; flexible curve
Right-angled triangle

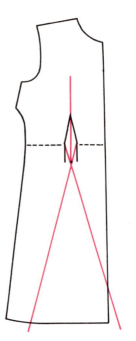

1 Mark the center point between the waist dart lines at the lower edge. Draw a line from this point to the waist dart point, extending it beyond the top of the dart as shown. Draw a line from waist level to hem from each side of the dart lines and through the center point.

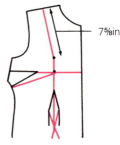

2 Continue the top bust dart line across to the center front. Redraw the lower bust dart line to the point where the two extended dart lines meet. From the center of the shoulder cutting line, measure down 7⅝in (19.5cm) to the extended waist dart line and mark.

3 Draw a line from this mark to the center front where it meets the extended bust dart line, and also to the side seamline where it meets the top bust dart line. All the style lines are now marked for the front and side front panels.

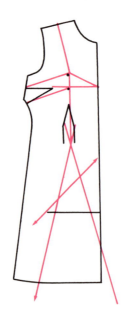

4 As the garment is to be cut on the bias, the grain lines have to be altered. Using a right triangle aligned to the center front, draw the new grain line at a 45° angle to the center front.

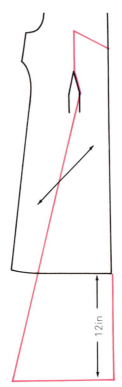

5 Trace the dress front panel, leaving a little extra paper at center front and enough at lower edge to lengthen hem by12in(30cm). Starting at the center front, trace the new neckline over the

bust to its highest point; continue down to the top point of the waist dart, along the waist dart inner stitching line to waist level, and finally down the extended line to the hem edge.

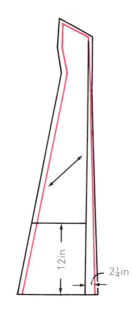

6 Measure out 2¼in (5.5cm) from the center front lower edge and mark. Join this mark to the waistline, tapering into the center front line. Add ⅝in (1.5cm) seam allowances all around the front panel, omitting the hem edge, which has a ¾in (2cm) allowance included.

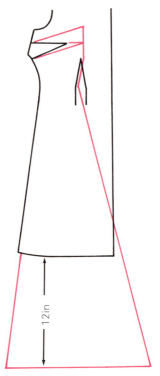

7 Trace the side front panel, lengthening the hem all around by 12in (30cm) as before. Starting from the side cutting line, trace the new neckline over the bust to the highest point; continue down the waist dart line to waist level, and finally down the extended line to the lower edge. Trace side cutting line from top of bust dart to extended hem edge.

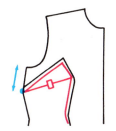

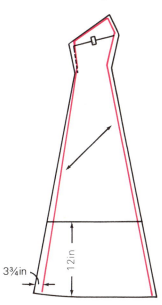

3¾in   12in

8 Cut along the top bust dart line and along the lower bust dart line to where these two lines meet. Close the dart opening with transparent tape, aligning the edges. The dart fullness has now been transferred to the seamline over the bust. To remove some of the fullness at the side seams, measure in 3¾in (9.5cm) at lower edge and redraw the side cutting line, tapering to waist level. Add ⅝in (1.5cm) seam allowances to side front panel, omitting hem and side edges.

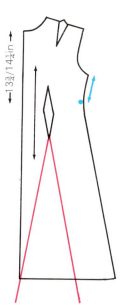

13¾/14¼in

9 To alter the dress back pattern, extend each waist dart line to the hem edge. Measure down the center back from the neck cutting line the following amount: for sizes 10 to 14: 13¾in (35cm); for sizes 16 to 20: 14¼in (36cm).

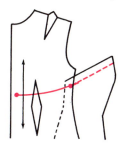

10 To determine the new back bodice line, measure down the side seam on the dress front from the cutting line at the armhole edge to the new side front bodice seamline. Mark this measurement on the side seam of the dress back, measuring down from the armhole cutting line.

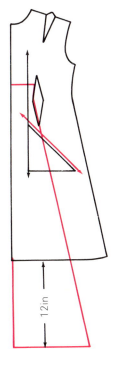

12in

11 Place the side front and side back together, matching bodice lines and marked points. Continue the neckline along from the side to the marked point at the center back. Use a flexible curve if necessary. The new line should cross the waist dart approximately 3½in (9cm) below the top dart point.

12 Mark the new grain line as before, aligning the right triangle to the original grain line and redrawing to a 45° angle. All the necessary style lines are now marked for the back patterns.

13 Trace the back panel, lengthening the hem by 12in (30cm). A ¾in (2cm) hem allowance is included in this measurement. Leave extra paper at center back edge. Trace new neckline from center back of bodice, across to first dart line; continue down dart line to waist, then down to lower edge.

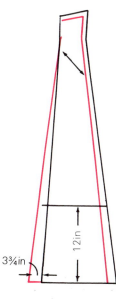

3¾in   12in

14 At the lower edge, extend the hem out from the center back by 3¾in (9.5cm). Draw the new center back cutting line, starting from the lower edge and tapering in to the original line at the waist. Add ⅝in (1.5cm) seam allowances to all edges except the hem edge and center back.

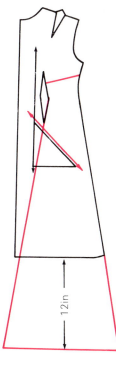

12in

15 Trace the side back panel the same way, following the new lines and lengthening hem by 12in (30cm).

John Hutchinson

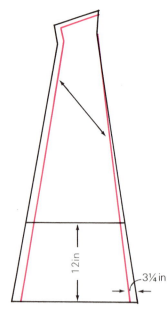

16 To reduce fullness at lower edge, measure in from side cutting line 3¼in (8.5cm) and draw new cutting line, tapering into original line at waist level. Add ⅝in (1.5cm) allowances all around, except side and hem edges.

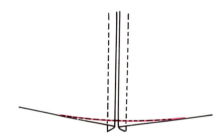

17 The angle of the hemline at the front and back inner seams will be too pointed and will need smoothing out. To do this, turn back the seam allowances of both edges and place the seamlines together, aligning the lower edges. Smooth out the point using a flexible curve and trim excess paper away.

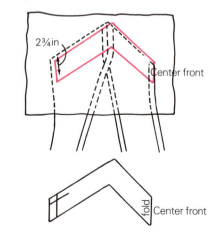

18 To cut a pattern for the front bodice facing, pin the dress front and side front panels together, overlapping to match the seamlines and aligning the top edges.

Trace the center front *seamline*, the top cutting line and the side cutting line. Make facing 2¾in (7cm) deep, curving inner angle slightly. The center front will be placed on a fold when cutting.

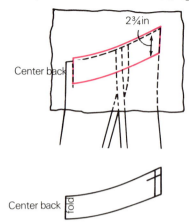

19 To cut the back bodice facing pattern, pin the dress back and side panels together, matching seamlines and top edges. Trace the center back *seamline*, the top cutting line and the side cutting line. Make the facing 2¾in (7cm) deep as before, noting that the center back is to be placed on a fold.

Note It is advisable to leave the cutting of the facing patterns until after the main garment has been cut out and fitted. If any adjustments need to be made, they can be transferred to the main pattern pieces before the facing pieces are cut.

Directions for making

Suggested fabrics
Lightweight, easily draped fabrics such as wool or silk crepe; for the lining: silk, rayon or synthetic taffeta, moiré, satin; for the appliqué: beads, sequins or fabrics on a net base.

Note A piece of elastic thread stitched under the back facing seam will give the bodice extra grip.
To prevent tube straps from stretching in wear, stitch a piece of seam binding in the seam before turning right side out.

Materials
54in (140cm)-wide fabric with or without nap:
    Sizes 10 to 14: 4⅝yd (4.2m)
    Sizes 16 to 20: 4⅞yd (4.4m)
36in (90cm)-wide interfacing:
    For all sizes: ½yd (.4m)
Matching thread
12in (30cm) zipper
2 cards bias binding (optional)
1 card seam binding
Elastic thread (optional)

Key to adjusted pattern pieces
A Dress front panel	Cut 2
B Dress side front panel	Cut 2
C Dress back panel	Cut 2
D Dress side back panel	Cut 2
E Front facing	Cut 1 on fold
F Back facing	Cut 1 on fold
Interfacing	
Use pieces E and F	Cut on fold

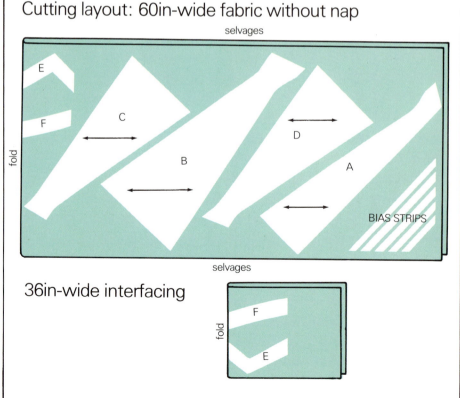

Cutting layout: 60in-wide fabric without nap

36in-wide interfacing

John Hutchinson

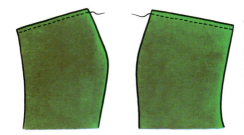

1 Prepare the fabric and cut out. Transfer all pattern markings to the fabric before removing the pattern. Staystitch the top edges of the dress.

2 With right sides together, pin and baste center front, side fronts, center back, side backs and side seams, leaving left side seam open 15¼in (38cm) from top edge. Baste 2¾in (7cm) from top edge; remaining opening of 12½in (31cm) is for zipper.

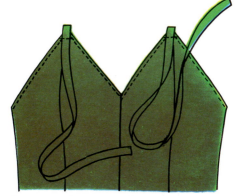

3 Cut two bias strips of fabric, each approximately 25in (64cm) long by 1in (2.5cm) wide. The length allows for adjustment. Make two tubing straps as directed in Volume 1, page 57. The finished straps should be about ¼in (6mm) wide; if necessary trim the seams to fit. Baste each strap to the upper points of the front, and leave the other ends free for adjustment.

4 The dress should be fitted at this stage, and you will need the help of another person. If the seams are to be adjusted, this must be done equally on every panel. For easy pinning, the initial fitting can be made with the garment tried on inside out, but final adjustments should be made with the garment right side out.

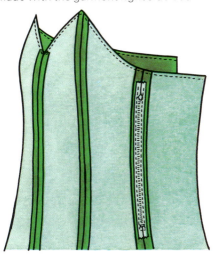

5 It is easier to put the zipper in with the dress laid out flat, so after fitting rip out the basting from one seam, first marking the seamline positions. Working from the lower edge up, stitch the seams, leaving the opening in one seam for the zipper. Finish the seams and press open. Insert the zipper into the side opening as directed in Volume 7, page 64. Stitch the remaining seam, finish and press open.

6 Baste interfacing to the wrong side of both facing pieces. With right sides together, baste and stitch the facings together at each side. Trim interfacing close to stitches. Press seams open. Finish lower edge of facings by overcasting or by turning ¼in (6mm) to wrong side and stitching in place.

7 Cross the straps over before basting them to the side back seams. With the straps hanging down onto the dress, pin and baste the facing in position on the top edges, matching the center front, center back and side seams. Try the dress on and check for strap adjustment; if this is satisfactory, stitch facings and straps in place. Apply seam binding to the

front facing seam as shown on page 61. For a snug fit, sew a piece of elastic thread or narrow elastic between facing and dress on the back seam.

8 Trim interfacing close to stitches. Grade the seam allowances and clip the front facing almost to the stitching at the center point. Trim off front points. Press the seam allowances toward the facing and understitch to the facing. Stitch into the front corners as far as possible. Press.

9 Turn the facings to the wrong side and catch-stitch to the center front, center back and side seams.

10 Leave the dress on a coat hanger for a few days. This will allow the hem to drop. Fit the dress hem carefully, leveling the hem edge and finishing with a tailor-bound hem as shown on page 62.

Terry Lewis

*Finishing the armhole edge
 of a lined jacket
*Applying a motif to a
 garment
*Lined bolero;
 adapting the pattern;
 directions for making

Finishing the armhole edge of a lined jacket

Lining a garment with sleeves can be a tricky procedure, as it may be difficult to match the armhole seams of the lining to those of the garment. The following method eliminates this problem because the sleeves and sleeve lining are attached to the armhole at the same time. The bodice or jacket lining is then finished over the armhole edge, which makes the whole garment easier to fit. As the seam allowances are pressed toward the main garment, and not toward the sleeve, it may be necessary to give the sleeve cap some "lift" by using a stiffener or padding, as for the bolero on page 70.

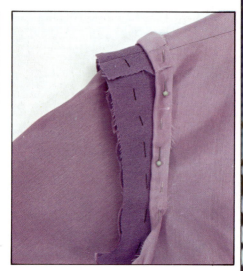

1 Make the garment body and sleeves and the linings, leaving the edges of the jacket free. Roll the lining back an inch or so (a few centimeters) around the armhole edge of the body and the sleeve cap and pin in place.

2 With right sides together (i.e. sleeve is right side out and main part is wrong side out, with the sleeve inside the main part of the jacket) and shoulder points, notches and underarm seams matching, pin and baste the sleeve to the armhole edge of the garment only, smoothing out fullness at sleeve cap by adjusting the gathers.

3 Stitch the seam, taking a ⅝in (1.5cm) seam allowance, making sure that the lining is not caught in the stitching.

4 Grade the seam and press toward the body of the garment, clipping curved edges so that the seam lies flat.

5 Turn in ⅝in (1.5cm) on the remaining raw edges at armholes on both lining pieces, clipping curves almost to the seamline. Slip stitch the lining in place so that all the raw edges of the armhole seams are enclosed.

Applying a motif to a garment

Motifs are usually applied to a garment before it is lined and are easier to apply if the garment is flat. If the motif covers several seams these must be stitched first. If the motif is heavily beaded, has a raised surface or is rather large, it will need to be sewn to the garment over its whole width and length to prevent its sagging. Slant basting (pad stitching) is the most suitable method for attaching a motif in the center area.

Various methods can be used to finish the edge of a motif, depending on the materials involved: a flat motif can be machine stitched in place with straight or close zig-zag stitch. Hand sewing is neater and gives a better finish to heavy appliqué, as can be seen on the bolero on page 70.

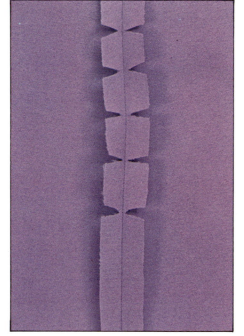

1 Baste, stitch and press any seams which will lie under the motif, so that the motif can be applied flat. Curved seams must be clipped and pressed open.

2 Pin remaining seams, pin motif to garment and try it on. Adjust position if necessary. Baste all around edge of the motif, about $\frac{5}{8}$in (1.5cm) in from raw edge of the backing net. If there is not enough net, baste close to edge of motif.

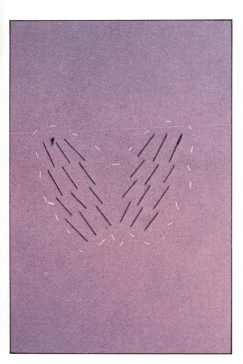

3 Working from the wrong side, make large diagonal tacking stitches across the area and very tiny straight stitches through to the motif. If the motif has a very raised surface, it may be easier to work from the right side, reversing the technique. Remove basting.

4 Most beaded or sequinned motifs have a net backing which is sewn to the garment. Turn under the edge of the backing fabric with the point of a needle and slip stitch or hem in place.

5 If there is not enough backing fabric to turn under, the raw edge must be finished with blanket or tiny herringbone stitch over the edge. For this sample we have left a wide border of net and used contrasting thread to show the stitches clearly.

Mike Berend

Lined bolero

This elegant short jacket with distinctive sleeves and an exotic motif is an ideal companion to the evening dress in the previous course.

Adapting the pattern

The bolero is made by adapting the pattern for the basic dress from the Stitch by Stitch Pattern Pack, available in sizes 10-20, which correspond to sizes 8-18 in ready-made clothes.

Materials
3 sheets of tracing paper 36×40in (90×100cm)
Flexible curve
Yardstick; right-angled triangle

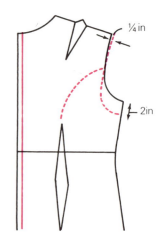

1 For the jacket back, trace the upper part of the dress back pattern, marking in the darts, lengthening and shortening line, and the grain line. Extend the shoulder line out by $\frac{1}{4}$in (6mm) and mark. Drop the armhole at the side seamline 2in (5cm) and mark. Using a flexible curve, redraw the armhole cutting line, joining these two points. The line will taper into the original cutting line at about the halfway point of the armhole edge.

2 Trim away the center back seam allowance, as the center back is placed on a fold. Draw the panel seamline from the halfway point of the armhole to the top point of the dart, using a flexible curve. Do not make the curve too deep.

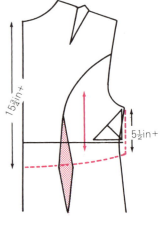

3 Extend the lengthening and shortening line slightly on the side seam cutting line.

Chris Harvey

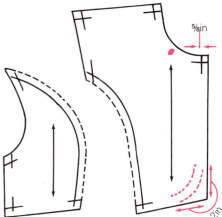

Using a triangle aligned with this line, draw the new side cutting line and extend it about an inch (a few centimeters) below the lengthening and shortening line. To mark length of the jacket, measure down center back from neck cutting line 15¾in (40cm) for a size 10, adding an extra ⅜in (1cm) to this measurement for each larger size.

4 To mark the length at the side seam, measure down from new armhole cutting line 5½in (14cm) for a size 10, adding an extra ¼in (6mm) for each larger size. Using a flexible curve, draw in new lower edge of jacket from center back to new side seam. A ⅝in (1.5cm) seam allowance is included. Mark grainline parallel to center back.

at the side seam by 2in (5cm) and mark.
7 Using a flexible curve, redraw the armhole cutting line from the new shoulder line to this mark. The shoulder line should taper into the original line about halfway down the armhole. Draw the new panel seamline from the halfway point at the armhole cutting line to the top of the dart, using a flexible curve. Do not make the curve too deep. Mark the grain line on both sections parallel to the center front.

10 Mark in all seamlines and add a ⅝in (1.5cm) seam allowance to each front section on the panel seamlines and also to the center front edge. Mark a point 2in (5cm) along the hem edge seamline from the center front, and a point 2in (5cm) up from the lower edge on the center front seamline. Using a flexible curve join these two points. Mark in the new cutting line on this curved edge, ⅝in (1.5cm) from the seamline.

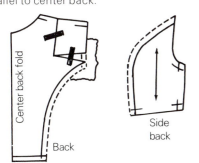

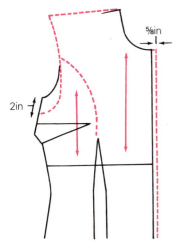

5 Cut along panel seamline and separate pattern, cutting from armhole through dart lines. The shaded area of the dart is trimmed away. To remove shoulder dart, cut the pattern from armhole to shoulder dart point and close up dart with tape. This will open the pattern at the armhole (to allow for shoulder pad). Tape paper under the slash and redraw armhole cutting line. Mark all seamlines, adding ⅝in (1.5cm) seam allowances to each back section on panel seam.

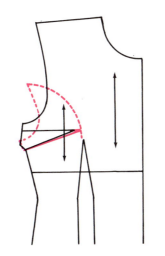

8 Extend the top bust dart line to the new panel seamline and redraw the lower bust dart line to this point. Cut along the panel seamline from the armhole to the top of the waist dart. Cut through and close the bust dart and tape in place.

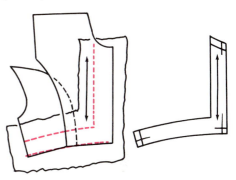

11 The lower and front edges of jacket have a 2¼in (5.5cm) interfacing. For front interfacing, pin front and side front together. Trace lower edge, smoothing out at panel seam. Make interfacing 2¼in (5.5cm) deep all around. This piece will be cut twice: once for each front.

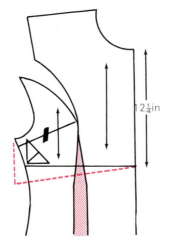

9 Using a triangle aligned with the lengthening and shortening line, redraw side seam cutting line as for the back. To mark the length of the jacket at center front, measure down from neck cutting line 12¼in (31cm) for a size 10, adding an extra ⅜in (1cm) for each larger size. To mark length at side seam, use the same measurement as on the back side seam. Continue cutting along the dart lines to the lower edge and separate the pattern pieces, trimming away the shaded area of the dart.

6 For the jacket front, trace the upper part of the dress front pattern, marking the darts, lengthening and shortening line and the grain line. Extend the armhole cutting line up by ⅜in (1cm) at shoulder point and redraw new shoulder line to neck edge. Extend this line out by ¼in (6mm) at shoulder point. Drop armhole

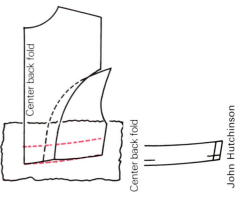

12 Repeat with the back and side back panels, marking the center back to be placed on a fold. Mark all seam allowances and grain lines on both the front and the back interfacing patterns.

John Hutchinson

71

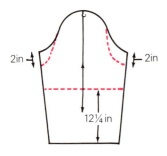

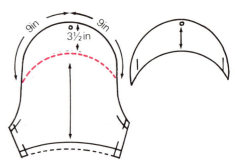

13 For the sleeve, trace the dress sleeve pattern and mark grain line. To mark the length, measure up from the lower edge 12¼in (31cm) and draw a line at right angles to the grain line across the pattern. Continue the grain line to the shoulder point. To drop armhole seam, measure down seamline at underarm curve 2in (5cm). Using flexible curve, redraw armhole curve on both sides. Mark new seam allowances all around.

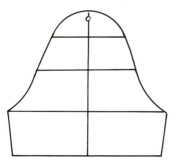

14 Draw a horizontal line across the pattern from cutting line to cutting line

at the underarm seam. Divide the remainder of the sleeve cap into three equal parts with horizontal lines. Before cutting the pattern, lay it over a sheet of paper so that it can be taped in place.

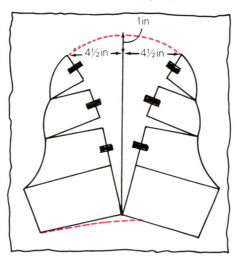

15 Cut down the center line of the sleeve to within ¼in (6mm) of hem edge. Cut out from the center on both sides of each horizontal line almost to the seamline, at the armhole edge. Spread the pattern up by about 1in (2.5cm), and out by about 4½in (11cm). Make sure both sides are equal before taping in place. Redraw the sleeve and curve the lower edge slightly in the center to smooth out the hemline. Redraw the grain line parallel to the center line.

16 To cut the pattern piece for the sleeve stiffener, measure down each side of the new sleeve cap from center point 9in (23cm). These marks will also represent the gathering points. Mark a point 3½in (9cm) down from sleeve cap and, using a flexible curve, join all points.

17 To make the collar pattern, use the stand collar from the Pattern Pack. Trace the collar pattern, making it ⅜in (1cm) wider at the top edge. The finished width of the collar will be 1⅝in (4cm). Mark the seamlines and the center back foldline.

Directions for making

Materials
- 60in (150cm)-wide fabric with or without nap:
  - Sizes 10, 12, 14, 16: 1⅛yd (1m)
  - Sizes 18, 20: 1¼yd (1.1m)
- Use the same widths and amounts for lining fabric, or if using 36in (90cm)-wide fabric for lining:
  - Sizes 10, 12: 1⅝yd (1.4m)
  - Sizes 14-20: 1¾yd (1.50m)
- 36in (90cm)-wide interfacing:
  - For all sizes: ⅝yd (.5m)
- Net or interfacing for sleeve cap:
- Matching thread
- 4⅜yd (4m) fine filler cord or ⅝yd (.5m) 60in (150cm)-wide contrasting fabric for cording (optional)
- Motif for shoulder and back or beads, sequins and net to make one

Key to adjusted pattern pieces
A Back	Cut 1 on fold
B Side back	Cut 2
C Front	Cut 2
D Side front	Cut 2
E Sleeve	Cut 2
F Collar	Cut 1

Lining:
Use pieces **A, B, C, D, E:** cut as for jacket
Interfacing:
Use pieces **A, B, C, D:** cut to lower and front edges.

Suggested fabrics
Lightweight wool or silk, crepe, polyester crepe; lining: taffeta, moiré, raw silk; motif: beads or sequins on net; heavy appliqué.

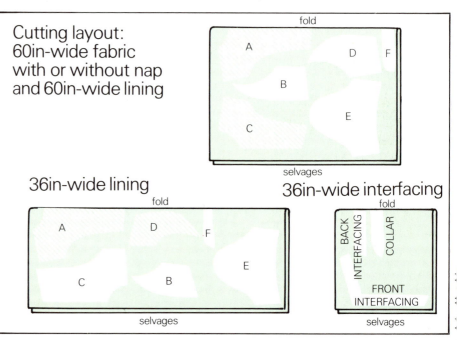

Cutting layout:
60in-wide fabric with or without nap and 60in-wide lining

36in-wide lining

36in-wide interfacing

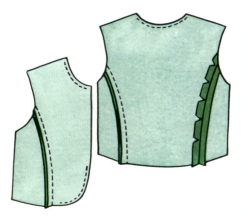

1 Prepare the main fabric and the lining fabric and cut out. Transfer all pattern markings to the fabric before removing the pattern. Stay stitch all curved edges. With right sides together, pin and baste fronts to side fronts and backs to side backs. Stitch seams, press open and clip curves where necessary.

2 With right sides together, baste and stitch jacket fronts to the back at the shoulder seams. Press seams open. Make shoulder pads as shown in Volume 9, page 60.
Apply to the shoulder part of the main garment from the wrong side, catch-stitching at shoulder and armhole seams.

Chris Harvey

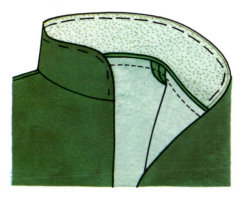

3 Baste the interfacing to the wrong side of the collar section (not to the collar lining). With right sides together, matching center backs, center fronts and shoulder points, baste and stitch collar to neck edge.

4 Trim the interfacing close to the stitching, clip the seam allowance around the neck edge and press the seam open. Position and apply the motif as shown on page 69. Baste and stitch side seams and press open.

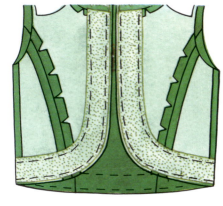
Terry Evans

5 Join front and back hem interfacings at the side seams. (Overlapping rather than making a flat seam at the seamline will give a smoother finish.) Baste the interfacing to the inside of the jacket at the hem and front edges. Catch-stitch to side seams.

6 Cut bias strips of fabric and join enough pieces to cord the outer edges of the collar, front and lower edge. Make the cording using a very fine cord and apply to jacket edges as directed in Volume 9, page 65.

7 Make the jacket lining, joining side front, side back, side and shoulder seams. Clip curves and press open. Attach lining collar to the neck of the lining body as directed for the jacket. Clip seam allowance and press open.

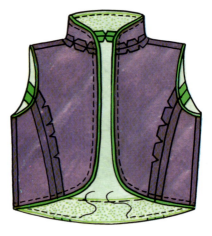

8 With right sides together, matching all outer edges and seams, pin the lining to the jacket. Baste and stitch the two parts together around collar, front and hem edges, leaving 6in (15cm) open at

center back for turning right side out. Do not stitch the armhole edges. Trim all interfacing close to the stitching. Grade seam allowances and clip curved edges. Press well.

9 Turn the jacket right side out through the back opening, and slip stitch the opening closed. Press. To hold the collar sections together at the neck seamline, slab stitch (close running stitch) them together through all thicknesses into the seamline at center back, shoulders and front edges. Make sure that all seamlines are positioned together.

10 Apply the net or interfacing to the sleeve cap of the main sleeve on the wrong side, matching shoulder point and

notches. With right sides together, join the underarm seam of the sleeves and press open. Do the same with the sleeve lining.

11 Cut bias strips to fit the hem edge of the sleeve and make cording. Apply the cording to the hem of the sleeve as in Volume 9, page 65. Slip the lining over the sleeve, with right sides together and all outer edges matching. Baste and machine stitch a $\frac{5}{8}$in (1.5cm) seam around the hem edge. Grade seam allowances; turn right side out and press lightly.

12 Matching raw edges and balance marks at the sleeve cap, machine stitch a row of gathering stitches between the notches at the sleeve cap just inside the seamline. Join the sleeve to the jacket and complete the lining as shown on page 68. Press seam gently.

*Conspicuous faced pockets
*Tailor's ham
*Pattern for yoked jacket:
 adapting the pattern;
 directions for making (1)

Conspicuous faced pockets

Facings are most often found on armholes and necklines and are used to finish and strengthen raw edges. Occasionally they are used elsewhere, such as on the pockets of the jacket on page 78. Here they are applied to the right side and are decorative as well as functional.

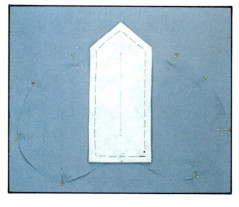

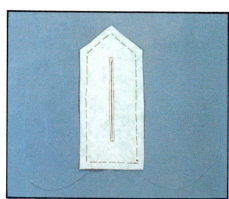

1 Transfer the pocket position to the garment, the pocket and pocket facing. With wrong sides together and pocket position lines matching, pin the pocket to the garment. Baste interfacing to wrong side of pocket facing. With interfaced side of facing up, and working from wrong side of garment, match pocket position lines. Pin and baste around outer edges through all thicknesses.

2 Stitch around pocket position $\frac{1}{8}$in (3mm) away from the center line, beginning at the center of one side and continuing around the marked line. Turn each corner by leaving the needle in the fabric raising the presser foot and pivoting the fabric. Cut through the center of the pocket to within $\frac{3}{8}$in (1cm) of each end. Cut diagonally into each corner without cutting through stitching lines.

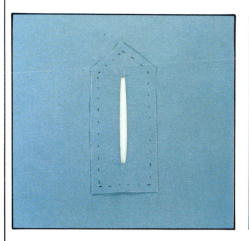

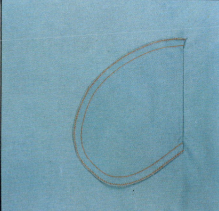

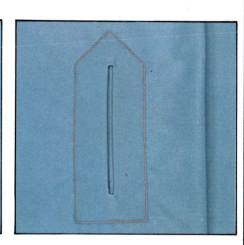

3 Pull pocket facing through the opening to right side of the garment. Square the corners of the facing seam allowances by pulling out triangular ends. Press ends and side seam allowances away from the opening. Press facing down flat over seams and press out any folds that form at the ends. On the inside, press both sides of pocket section toward center front edge. Pin and baste pocket halves together.

4 Trim the lower piece to same shape as upper part. Baste and stitch around the outer edge of the pocket, taking a $\frac{5}{8}$in (1.5cm) seam allowance. Finish the outer edges by overcasting them together by hand or machine. Do not catch the right side of the garment in the pocket stitching. Press.

5 On the right side, turn under $\frac{5}{8}$in (1.5cm) around the outer edge of the pocket facing. Press/trim the raw edges slightly and clip the points so that the facing will lie flat. Pin and baste the facing to the garment only, not to the pocket piece inside. Topstitch around the facings, stitching close to the edge.

Mike Berend

Tailor's ham

DART SEAM LINE

fold

cut 2

cut 1 (double)

center seam

DART SEAM LINE

Tailor's hams are a useful aid to pressing. Pressing over a ham placed inside a garment prevents marks from forming on the right side of the garment when seams and darts are pressed hard.

The photographs at the bottom of the page show the finished ham, from the top and the side. One end of the ham has a large curve, which is useful for pressing large sleeve caps; the other end has a smaller, pointed curve for awkward areas. The curve is placed under a seam and the seam pressed over it. There is also a dart made in the ham which can be placed under a dart on the garment so that the dart can be pressed over it.

Traditionally hams were shaped bags of muslin or fine wool with a firm stuffing and were not washable. For general home use, a ham shape made of polyester fiberfill stuffed very tightly with shredded foam and then covered with undyed muslin is most suitable, as this can be washed occasionally.

Tailor's hams can be any size, but the most useful is one which is easy to handle and which will fit into specific areas of a garment.

On this page are trace patterns and directions for making a ham of convenient size and shape.

1 Cut out the ham shapes in fiberfill. Close darts and stitch, taking $\frac{3}{8}$in (1cm) seams. Join center seam taking $\frac{3}{8}$in (1cm) seam.
2 Place ham sections together with right sides facing and notches matching. Stitch all around taking a $\frac{3}{8}$in (1cm) seam, leaving open area on one side between notches for turning right side out.
3 Turn right side out and stuff hard with shredded foam. Slip stitch the opening closed.
4 Cut out and make a muslin bag in the same way, leaving open the whole side seam. Push the padded bag inside, easing into place and matching darts. Slip stitch the opening closed.

Yoked jacket

This casual, loose-fitting jacket with a gathered yoke looks good with tapered slacks and a top or with a dress.

Adapting the pattern

The jacket is made by adapting the pattern for the basic shirt from the Stitch by Stitch Pattern Pack, available in sizes 10-20, which correspond to sizes 8-18 in ready-made clothes.

Materials

4 sheets of tracing paper 36 × 40in (approx. 90 × 100cm)
Flexible curve; right-angled triangle Yardstick

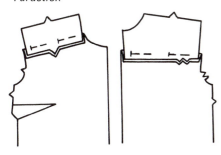

1 Pin the front yoke to the shirt front and the back yoke to the shirt back, overlapping the seam allowances so that the seamlines are aligned. Trace front and back pieces, leaving extra paper at the center front and center back edges.
2 On the front pattern, extend the shoulder line up by $\frac{1}{4}$in (6mm), move it in by $\frac{3}{8}$in (1cm) and mark. Starting at the marked point and using a triangle aligned with the new shoulder line, draw the armhole yoke line, which will be at a right angle to the shoulder line. Continue this line down, ending a couple of inches above the bust dart.

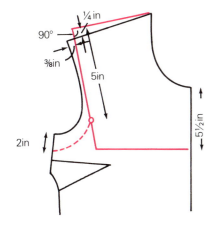

3 Measure down this line 5in (12.5cm) from the shoulder cutting line and mark

with a circle. Drop the armhole by 2in (5cm) at the side seam and, using a flexible curve, connect this point to the circle on the armhole seam.
4 For bust yoke line, measure down center front from neck cutting line, 5$\frac{1}{2}$in (14cm) for sizes 10 and 12; 6in (15cm) for sizes 14 and 16; 6$\frac{1}{4}$in (16cm) for sizes 18 and 20. Draw a line across pattern at a right angle to center front line to meet extended armhole yoke line.
5 Add 4in (10cm) to width at center front edge, from yoke line down to lower edge. For the collar extension at the center front neck edge, extend neck cutting line at center front by $\frac{5}{8}$in (1.5cm). Draw a line from this point, tapering into the center front at the yoke line.
6 Draw the yoke curve at the inner corner using a flexible curve. For the gathering position, measure down 2in (5cm) from the first circle, following the curve, and mark another circle. Draw a line up to the yoke line from point of the bust dart, parallel to center front line.

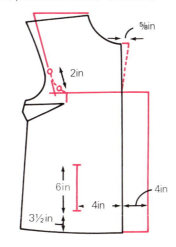

7 For pocket position, measure up 3$\frac{1}{2}$in (9cm) from lower edge and in 4in (10cm) from original center front line. Draw a line up from this point parallel to center front, and 6in (15cm) long.

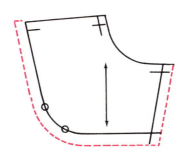

8 Cut along the yoke line from the front edge to the armhole, following the curve and continuing up to the new shoulder line. Add a $\frac{5}{8}$in (1.5cm) seam allowance to front edge and to the new yoke seamline. Mark the grainline parallel to the original center front line.

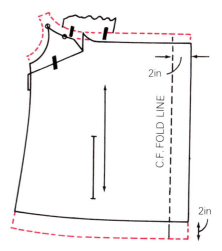

9 On the front section, cut down the marked line from yoke to bust dart point. Close the dart and tape in place. This will open the pattern. Tape a piece of paper behind the slash and straighten the yoke seamline. Add a $\frac{5}{8}$in (1.5cm) seam allowance to the armhole and yoke line. Mark the front facing foldline 2in (5cm) in from the front edge. Add 2in (5cm) to lower edge for the hem allowance.

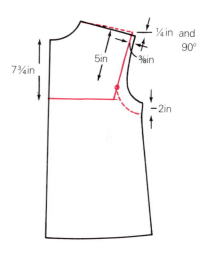

10 On the back pattern, measure down center back from neck cutting line 7$\frac{3}{4}$in (19.5cm) for sizes 10 and 12; 8in (20.5cm) for sizes 14 and 16; 8$\frac{1}{2}$in (21.5cm) for sizes 18 and 20. Draw a line from this point across the pattern to the armhole edge, at a right angle to the center back. This is the back yoke line.
11 Extend the shoulder line up by $\frac{1}{4}$in (6mm) and move in by $\frac{3}{8}$in (1cm), marking this point. Starting at this point, draw the new armhole yoke line to meet the back yoke line, using a triangle aligned with the new shoulder line. The armhole yoke line will be at a right angle to the shoulder line.
12 Measure down this line 5in (12.5cm) and mark with a circle. Drop the armhole by 2in (5cm) at side seam and, using a flexible curve, join this point to the circle to mark the new armhole seamline.

John Hutchinson

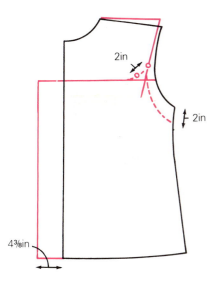

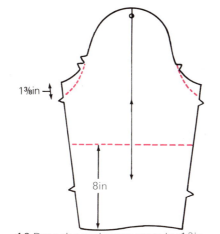

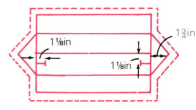

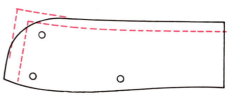

21 Mark a buttonhole on each pointed section on the same side, 1⅛in (3cm) from center foldline and ⅛in (3mm) longer than diameter of the button. Add ⅝in (1.5cm) seam allowances all around.

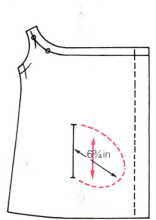

22 For the collar, trace the shirt collar band on paper. Straighten the front edge, keeping the line parallel to the center front, and mark the seam allowances.

13 Add 4⅜in (11cm) to width at center back edge from the yoke line down to the lower edge. Draw the new yoke curve at the inner corner using a flexible curve. For the gathering position, measure down 2in (5cm) from first circle, following curve, and mark a second circle.

16 Drop the underarm seam by 1⅜in (3.5cm) on each side of the sleeve and, using a flexible curve, redraw the underarm curves from the marked points tapering into the notches.

17 Draw a line across the pattern at right angles to the grainline and level with the underarm cutting lines. Divide the sleeve into four equal parts, using the center line as a guide. Before cutting the pattern, lay it over a piece of pattern paper so that it can be taped in place immediately.

18 Cut along all three lines. Using the horizontal line as a guide to keep pattern straight, spread pattern out by equal amounts of 2⅜in (6cm) at top and 2¾in (7cm) at lower edge. Tape pattern down.

23 To make the pocket pattern, draw the shape of the pocket on the jacket front as shown, using a flexible curve. The pocket should be 6¾in (17cm) deep and should slant downward. Mark the grainline parallel to the pocket position.

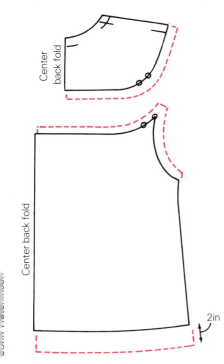

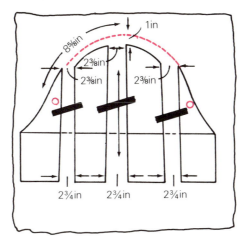

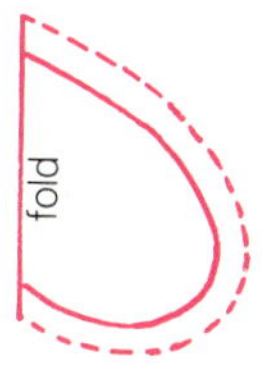

14 Cut along the yoke line to separate the pattern pieces. Add a ⅝in (1.5cm) seam allowance to the outer edge of the yoke and to the yoke edge and armhole edge of the back section. Add 2in (5cm) to the lower edge for the hem allowance.

15 For the sleeve, trace the shirt sleeve pattern and mark in the grainline. To mark the sleeve length, measure up from the lower edge 8in (20cm) and draw a line across the pattern at right angles to the grainline. This measurement includes a ⅝in (1.5cm) seam allowance at the lower edge. Continue the grainline to the top of the sleeve cap.

19 Redraw the sleeve cap, making it 1in (2.5cm) higher in the center than original cutting line. Mark the seam allowance. For the gathering positions, measure around sleeve cap 8⅝in (22cm) along each side from the center of the sleeve, and mark with circles. Draw the grainline parallel to the center line.

20 To make cuff pattern, draw a rectangle 12×10in (30×25cm) for size 10; for each larger size add ⅜in (1cm) to each of these measurements. Divide rectangle lengthwise into four equal parts. Extend center line by 1¾in (4.5cm) at each end. Join the point at each end to the two outer marked lines of the center as shown.

24 Trace the pocket shape and add a ⅝in (1.5cm) seam allowance around the curved edge only. The straight edge is placed on the fold.

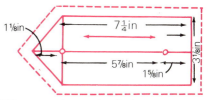

25 To make the pocket facing pattern, draw a rectangle 3⅛×7¼in (8×18.5cm).

Draw a line through center of rectangle and extend top end by $1\frac{1}{8}$in (3cm). Join this point to each side of rectangle. From lower edge, measure up center line $1\frac{5}{8}$in (4cm) and mark length of pocket position. Add a $\frac{5}{8}$in (1.5cm) seam allowance to all edges. Mark grainline parallel to center line.

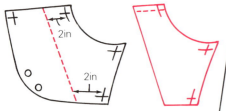

26 To make the front yoke interfacing pattern, measure 2in (5cm) along shoulder seamline from neck seamline and 2in (5cm) along lower edge from center front. Connect the two points. Trace this shape on paper and mark the seam allowances. If using woven interfacing, mark the grainline on the pattern.

Chris Harvey

Directions for making (1)

Suggested fabrics
Heavy- to medium-weight cottons such as denim, broadcloth, poplin, sailcloth; medium-weight fabrics with a sheen such as cotton satin or taffeta.

Materials
45in (115cm)-wide fabric without nap:
   Sizes 10, 12: $3\frac{1}{2}$yd (3.1m)
   Sizes 14, 16: $3\frac{5}{8}$yd (3.3m)
   Sizes 18, 20: $3\frac{3}{4}$yd (3.4m)
36in (90cm)-wide interfacing:
   For all sizes: $\frac{3}{4}$yd (.7m)
Matching thread
3 sets button-link fastenings and 2 matching buttons; or 8 buttons

Key to adjusted pattern pieces
A	Jacket front	Cut 2
B	Jacket back	Cut 1 on fold
C	Front yoke	Cut 2
C	Front yoke facing	Cut 2
D	Back yoke	Cut 1 on fold
D	Back yoke facing	Cut 1 on fold
E	Sleeve	Cut 2
F	Cuff	Cut 2
G	Collar band	Cut 2 on fold

H	Pocket	Cut 2 on fold
I	Pocket facing	Cut 2
J	Front yoke interfacing	Cut 2

Interfacing: Use pieces G, F (cut half width only); I, A (cut to front facing width only) and J.

Cutting layout: 45in-wide fabric without nap

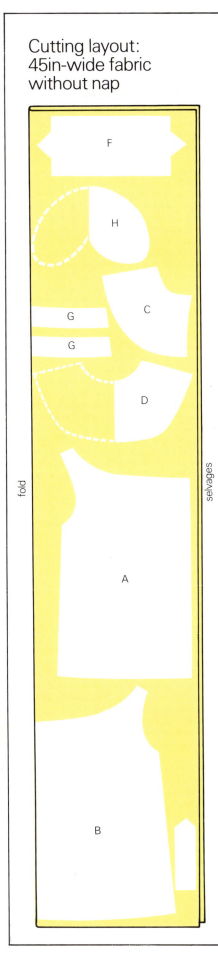

1 Prepare the fabric and cut out. Transfer all pattern markings to the fabric before removing the pattern. Staystitch all curved edges.

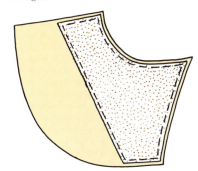

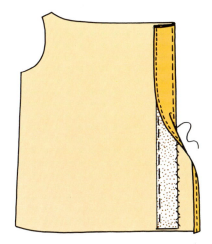

2 Baste the interfacing to the wrong side of the front yokes and the jacket fronts. Catch-stitch the interfacing to the center front foldlines of the jacket fronts.

3 Finish edge of long front facings by turning in ¼in (6mm) and machine stitching. Press. Turn the front facings to the inside and baste in place. Press.

36in-wide interfacing

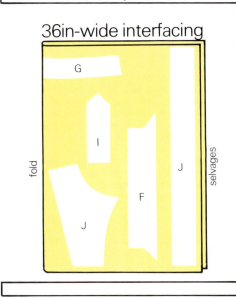

4 Mark pocket positions on both jacket fronts and make conspicuous faced pockets as shown on page 75.

45in-wide fabric without nap

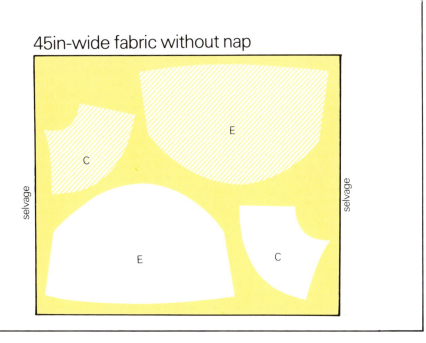

Terry Evans

John Hutchinson

*Making and applying a
 turned-back cuff
*Button-link fastenings
*Pattern for yoked jacket:
 directions for making (2)

Making and applying a turned-back cuff

Cuffs are often plain, but they can also be decorative—an integral part of the design, lending an air of distinction as do the turned-back cuffs on the jacket on page 84. This kind of cuff is usually applied with a split band and often has a button-link fastening.

1 Transfer the fold line positions from pattern to cuff section. Baste the interfacing to half of the cuff and catch-stitch it to the center fold line. Baste along the outer fold line.

2 Put the cuff ends together with the right sides inside. Baste and stitch seams to the outer fold lines, leaving the pointed section unstitched. Anchor the ends of the stitching and clip seam allowances almost to the stitching line. Trim the interfacing close to the stitching. Press seams open.

3 Push one half of the cuff through the other and fold on the center line. Bring the pointed pieces together with right sides together. Baste and stitch across from one point to the other without catching in previous stitching. Anchor; clip across corners. Trim interfacing.

4 Turn the cuff right side out. Baste close to the folded edge. Press flat. Make a buttonhole on each side of the cuff in the position shown on the pattern drawing (see page 86).

5 To position the cuff correctly on the lower edge of the sleeve, fold the cuff in half and mark with a tailor's tack at the fold opposite the pointed end. This tack will match the underarm seam of the sleeve; the seam at the pointed end will match the center of the sleeve.

6 Make the sleeve and run two rows of gathering stitches around the lower edge. With right sides together and marked points matching, pin the cuff to the sleeve at the underarm seam and the center. Pull up the gathering threads until the sleeve fits. Spread the gathers evenly and pin in place. Baste on the seamline.

7 Stitch the cuff to the sleeve with the sleeve on top. Grade the seam allowances. Remove basting. Press seam allowance toward the cuff.

8 On the inside of the sleeve, turn under $\frac{5}{8}$in (1.5cm) on the inner edge of the cuff. Press. Baste and then slip stitch the cuff to the stitching line. Press. The cuff is now ready to be turned back and fastened with button links.

Button-link fastenings

These are used instead of cuff links or at an edge-to-edge fastening elsewhere on a garment. Generally the buttonholes are hand-worked and positioned horizontally, with a round end nearest the opening to take the strain.

The links can be made by joining decorative buttons; the flat type of button with central holes and no shank is the easiest to use. The threads over the holes in the buttons can be rubbed with beeswax for additional strength.

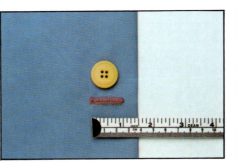

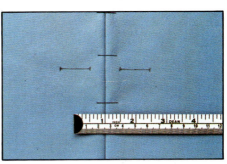

1 Measure the button diameter and make a horizontal buttonhole on both sides of the garment; allow a fraction of an inch for ease. The holes should be positioned half the diameter of the button from the edge.

2 Close the opening and baste it flat. The distance from the center of one buttonhole to the center of the other will be the finished length of the link.

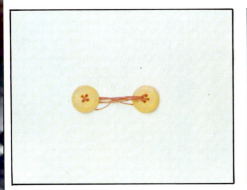

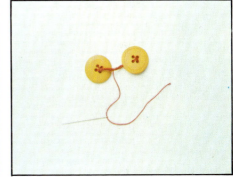

3 Using button thread double or mercerized crochet cotton, join the two buttons with a crossover link and a reef knot. The link should be a little longer than the required finished length. Trim the ends of the knot and move it to the center.

4 Thread the needle with a single thickness thread and, leaving a short end, take it from the back of one button over the front and through another hole to the back of the same button.

5 Work a line of blanket or buttonhole stitch along the link over all threads and ends to the other end. Take the thread through to the front of the second button and back again, finishing carefully with tiny backstitches into the link behind the button.

Simon Butcher

83

Yoked jacket

This loose-fitting jacket looks great over slacks or a pretty dress.
The directions which started on page 72 continue on the next
page. Directions for making the coordinated dress start in the
next courses in the next volume.

Chris Harvey

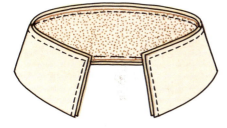

4 With right sides together, baste and stitch the shoulder seams of the yokes and yoke facings. Trim the interfacing close to the stitching. Press the seams open.

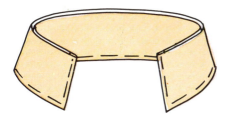

5 Baste the interfacing to the wrong side of one collar piece. With right sides together and edges even, baste and stitch the two sections together, leaving the neck edge open.

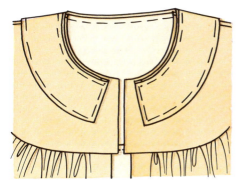

6 Trim the interfacing and seam allowances and clip corners. Turn the collar right side out. Baste around the outer edges and press.

Directions for making (2)

1 Run two rows of gathering stitches along the yoke seamline on the jacket fronts and back, stitching from the circles to the front facing on the jacket fronts, and between the circles on the back section.

2 With right sides together and center fronts and circles matching, pin the jacket fronts to the front yokes, pulling up the gathering threads until the jacket fits the yoke. Baste, spreading the gathers evenly. Repeat for the jacket back.

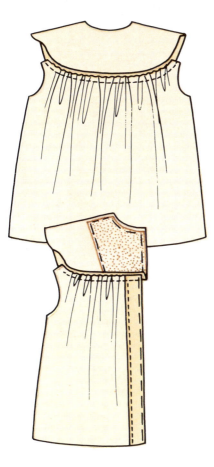

3 Stitch the yoke seams of the jacket back and fronts. Trim the interfacings close to the stitching line. Press the seam allowances toward the yokes on all three pieces.

7 With the interfaced side of the collar next to the neck edge, baste the collar to this edge through all thicknesses, matching fronts and shoulder points.

8 With right sides together, stitch shoulder seams of yoke facings and press open.

9 With right sides together and center backs, front edges and shoulder seams matching, baste and stitch the front and back yoke facings to the front and back yokes, stitching around neck edge and along front edges of the yoke seamlines.

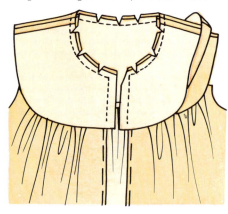

10 Trim the interfacing close to the stitching at the neck edge. Grade the seam allowances and clip curves. Clip across the front corners. Press well.

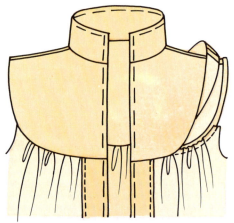

11 Turn the yoke facing to the inside of the jacket and baste around the neck edge. Press. The inside is not finished until the sleeves have been set in.

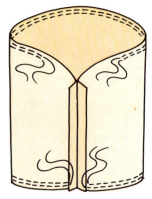

12 Run two rows of gathering stitches around the sleeve cap between the

circles. With right sides together, baste and stitch the underarm seam and press open. Run two rows of gathering stitches around the lower edge of the sleeve.

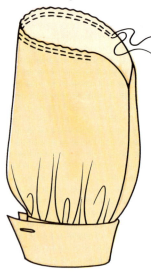

13 Make the turn-back cuff and attach it to the lower edge of the sleeve as shown on page 83. Complete the buttonholes and fasten with button-link fastenings. Make the second sleeve.

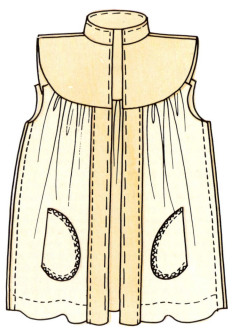

14 With right sides together, baste and stitch the side seams of the jacket. Press seams open. Try on the jacket to check the length and mark the hemline with a row of basting. Trim the lower edge so hem allowance is 2in (5cm) deep.

15 With right sides together and underarm seams, circles and shoulder points matching, pin the sleeve into the armhole, pulling up the gathering threads until the sleeve fits. Baste, spreading the gathers evenly.

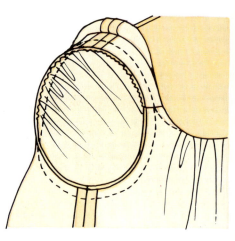

16 The sleeve is inserted in two stages. The first stitching is taken over the sleeve cap from circle to circle, with the seam allowance of the yoke facing folded back out of the way. Then the lower curve of the armhole is stitched from back to front. This allows the upper seam to be turned up into the yoke.

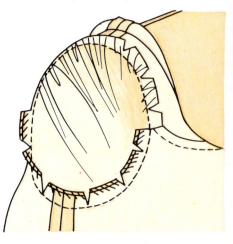

17 Clip the seam allowances around the armhole and press them toward the jacket. Finish the seam allowances of the lower armhole edge by overcasting them together.

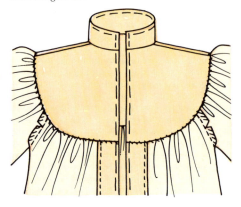

18 Turn under $\frac{5}{8}$in (1.5cm) around the entire outer edge of the yoke facing. Press. Pin the facing to the yoke, enclosing all raw edges. Baste and slip stitch to the stitching line. Press.

21 On the right side of the jacket fronts, topstitch ¼in (6mm) in from edge and another 1⅛in (3cm) in, beginning the stitching at the yoke seamline and stitching to the lower edge. Press.

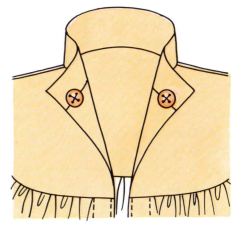

22 Turn the collar back and sew a button on each side, sewing through all thicknesses of jacket to hold the collar back. Position the buttons on the neck seamline.

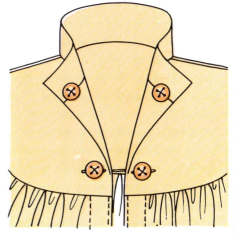

23 Make a horizontal buttonhole, ½in (1.3cm) up from the yoke seamline and ⅝in (1.5cm) in from the center front on each side of the jacket fronts. Fasten with button-links (see page 83).

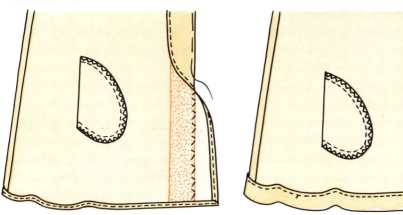

19 Turn the front facings out at the lower edge of the jacket fronts. Trim 2in (5cm) off bottom of front interfacings. Finish the raw edge of the hem by turning under ¼in (6mm) and stitching. Press.

20 Turn up hem and baste close to fold line. Sew hem to jacket with invisible hemming. Turn the facing to the inside of the jacket and slip stitch to the hem allowance. Remove basting and press the folded edge of the hem only.

Needlework / COURSE 14

Machine embroidery

You do not need a machine that does decorative stitches in order to do machine embroidery. On the contrary, the most creative work—called "free motion embroidery"—is done using just straight stitch and zig-zag, varying the stitch size, tension and thread for interesting effects.

Materials for machine embroidery

Threads Special machine embroidery thread is available; it is more flexible and lustrous than ordinary thread, and finer. For example, a 50 machine embroidery thread is finer than a 50 ordinary thread. This size and size 30, which is thicker, are suitable for most purposes. A size 14 machine needle can be used with either. Once you become skilled at controlling the machine you can use heavier threads in the needle, provided they will go through the eye without breaking. You can also use various interesting threads in the bobbin.

Fabrics Many different fabrics can be used for machine embroidery. Experienced embroiderers work with fine net and even chiffon, but when you are learning, it is best to use firmly-woven fabrics, such as poplin, denim or gabardine. Always buy extra fabric to practice on.

Frames Keeping the fabric taut is vitally important in machine embroidery, and for this an embroidery hoop is essential. One with an 8in (20cm) diameter is most useful; it should have a screw adjustment. A thin one, especially designed for machine work, will slip under the needle easily; otherwise you may need to remove the presser bar when placing the work on the machine. Bind the inner ring with seam tape or seam binding to help prevent the fabric from slipping.

Adjusting the machine

For free motion embroidery remove the presser foot and either lower the feed dog or cover it with the plate provided with some machines. (See the instruction booklet for your machine.) These adjustments permit you to move the fabric in any direction you like. You will also need to loosen the tension on both the upper thread and the bobbin; the former should usually be slightly looser than the latter. You may need to re-adjust the tension several times before it is right for your fabric and thread.

Quite a bit of practice is needed for free motion machine embroidery. Once you remove the presser foot and the feed dog, you must assume their controlling functions, which can feel very awkward at first. You'll probably need at least 10 hours of fairly intensive practice before you can work harmoniously with the machine. Start with a piece of finely-woven cotton and machine embroidery thread and proceed as shown below until you can work smoothly.

Working free motion embroidery

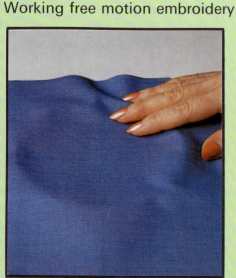

1 Adjust the screw on the frame's outer ring so that it fits smoothly over the inner ring. Remove the inner ring and place the fabric over the outer ring.

2 Place the inner ring on top and press it down with the heels of your hands until it grips securely. If there are any wrinkles in the fabric, gently pull the free edges of the fabric back over the outer ring to smooth them out. Tighten the screw if necessary and press the inner ring slightly below the outer.

3 Wind the bobbin and thread the machine as usual. Raise the needle, slide the frame under the needle and then lower the presser bar, as you would if the foot were attached; this engages the tension. Holding onto the thread, turn the wheel to lower the needle into the fabric and pick up the bobbin thread.

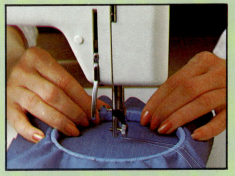

4 Hold both threads with one hand and again lower the needle into the same hole. Make a few stitches to anchor the threads, then cut the thread ends.

5 Place the thumbs on the outside of the hoop and the first three fingers on the cloth, well away from the needle. Keep your wrists relaxed and don't let your arms rest on the machine or table.

6 Press the foot control at a medium speed and move the frame steadily away from you, then back toward you. Continue stitching forward and backward, keeping the needle speed and the movement of the frame as smooth as possible. Repeat, working from side to side.

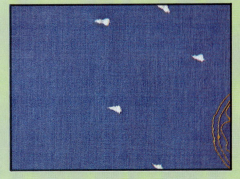

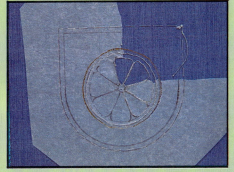

7 Once you feel confident about stitching in straight lines, try stitching spirals and circles. These may be irregular to start with but will improve with practice.

8 For satin stitch, set the machine for the closest zig-zag stitch and feed the fabric through relatively slowly. With practice you can adjust the width of the stitch with the right hand while moving the frame with the left.

9 When working a motif, you can first baste a tracing to the fabric and stitch the main lines through the paper. Then tear away the paper and fill in parts of the design with appropriate stitching.

Causes of thread breaking

Beginners in machine embroidery generally find that the upper thread breaks frequently. This has several possible causes. Among the most common are:

An incorrectly-threaded machine.
A blunt needle.
A too-fine needle that frays the thread.

Letting the machine stitch too quickly in the same place.
Moving the frame too quickly.
The fabric not being sufficiently taut.

Oranges and lemons . . .

. . . decorate this simple dirndl skirt. They'd look just as good on a tote bag or a pair of shorts.

Size
The finished skirt has a 22in (56cm) waistband and measures 13½in (34cm) in length. A seam allowance of ⅝in (1.5cm) is included.

Materials
1yd (1m) of 45in (115cm)-wide cotton poplin or similar fabric
Machine embroidery thread, size 30,
in yellow, orange and white (shaded orange thread was used on the skirt shown)
An 8in (20cm)-diameter embroidery hoop
Lightweight interfacing for waistband
Tissue paper
Matching sewing thread
A 5in (13cm) zipper
2 hooks and eyes

Michael Joseph / designed by Jennifer Gray

Working the embroidery

1 Cut out the pieces for the skirt: one piece the width of the fabric × 15½in (40cm), a waistband 3¾in (9.5cm) wide and 24¼in (62cm) long (or required waistband measurement), and two square pocket pieces 4in (10cm) larger than the diameter of the hoop.

2 Trace motif A on a piece of tissue paper, omitting the pocket edges.

3 Mount a piece of the extra fabric in the frame (see page 88) for practicing.

Baste the tracing to the fabric.

4 Thread the machine with white machine embroidery thread and prepare to stitch (see page 88). Stitch a few lines forward and backward on one side of the motif in order to check the tension; adjust if necessary.

5 Using a very short straight stitch, work around the inner circle of the motif and then around each orange section. Where the sections meet, stitch the second line over the first if possible, to create a continuous line. Using orange thread,

stitch the outer line.

6 Tear away the tissue paper, making sure to remove it completely.

7 Using white thread and straight stitch, fill in the area between the inner white line and the orange sections.

8 Thread the machine with orange (or shaded orange) thread and fill in the sections. Begin with a few straight stitches to anchor the thread, then set the machine to the widest zig-zag stitch and work back and forth until one section is filled. Finish with a few straight stitches, then move on to the next section.

9 Satin stitch around the outer edge, covering the straight-stitched orange line, using orange thread and a medium width stitch. Turn the frame slightly while stitching so that the stitches are aligned with the center.

10 Finally, using white thread and satin stitch, work a few seeds in the center. Vary the width of the stitch as you go to shape them.

11 Continue practicing until you can embroider the motif smoothly. Also practice the lemons in motif B. Remember to keep the fabric taut in the frame; this helps to prevent puckering. If the fabric does pucker, steam press the completed motif on both sides.

12 Now work the embroidery for the skirt. Trace motif A, including the pocket edges, and baste it, along the pocket outline, to the framed pocket piece. Work the embroidery as in steps 4-10. When removing the tissue, leave the basting threads in the fabric.

13 Fold the skirt fabric in half to find the center front panel (parallel to selvages).

Baste along this line.

14 Trace motif B. Baste the tracing to the skirt, positioning it so that the center of the top lemon slice is $5\frac{1}{2}$in (14cm) to the right of the center front and 7in (18cm) from the lower edge of the fabric.

15 Work the embroidery. The vertical lemon section is stitched in much the same way as the slices but with several white lines down the center and wide zig-zag stitched horizontally.

16 Press the embroidery on the wrong side over a folded towel.

Assembling the skirt

1 Run two gathering threads along the upper edge of the skirt.

2 Placing right sides together, pin and stitch the center back seam up to a point 6in (15cm) from the top. Baste the seam above this point.

3 Insert the zipper, following the manufacturer's instructions.

4 Cut a piece of interfacing the size of the waistband. Baste or iron it to the wrong side of the waistband. Fold the waistband in half, right sides facing, and stitch

across both ends. Trim seams and turn waistband right side out.

5 Pull up the gathering threads until the skirt measures 1in (2.5cm) less than the waistband. Adjust the gathers evenly and pin one side of the waistband to the skirt, right sides and raw edges matching, leaving a 1in (2.5cm) waistband underlap on the right-hand side. Baste and stitch in place. Grade the seam allowances.

6 Fold the other edge of the waistband over the raw edges and slip stitch it in place. Also slip stitch the lower edges of the underlap. Sew on hooks and eyes.

7 Baste the two pocket pieces together, right sides facing. Stitch along the original line of basting, leaving a small gap in the upper edge. Trim the seam allowances to $\frac{3}{8}$in (1cm), clip curves and turn pocket right side out. Press. Slip stitch the gap edges together. Topstitch along the upper edge.

8 Pin the pocket to the skirt in desired position. Baste and topstitch in place.

9 Turn up $1\frac{1}{2}$in (4cm) along lower edge. Zig-zag stitch the raw edge, baste in place and hem.

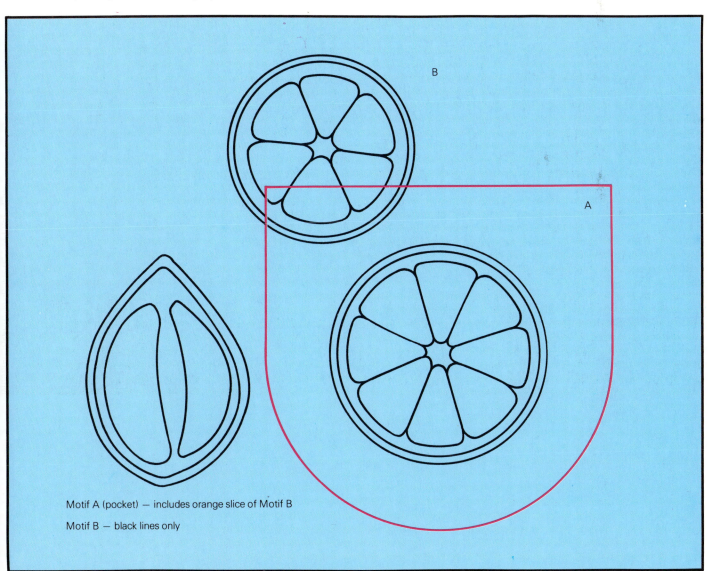

Motif A (pocket) — includes orange slice of Motif B

Motif B — black lines only

Ace of diamonds

Stylish slipovers to crochet for men and women. Add extra flair with a contrasting diamond motif.

Sizes

To fit 32[34:36:38:40:42]in (83[87:92:97:102:107]cm) bust/chest.
Length, 23¾[24:24¾:25¾:26½:26¾]in (60[61:63:65:67:68]cm).
Note Directions for larger sizes are in brackets []; if there is only one set of figures it applies to all sizes.

Materials

9[9:9:11:11:11]oz (250[250:250: 300:300:300]g) of a sport yarn in main color (A)
2oz (50g) in each of 2 contrasting colors (B and C)
Size E (3.50mm) crochet hook
1 pair No. 2 (2¾mm) knitting needles

Gauge

18dc to 4in (10cm) on size E (3.50mm) hook.

Back

Using size E (3.50mm) hook and A, make 85[89:95:99:103:109]ch.
Base row 1dc into 4th ch from hook, 1dc into each ch to end. Turn.
Patt row 3ch to count as first dc, 1dc into each dc to end. Turn. 83[87:93:97:101:107]dc.**
This row forms patt. Cont in patt until work measures 13½[13¾:13¾:14¼:14¼: 14½]in (34[35:35:35:36:36:37]cm).

Sizes 32[34:36]in (83[87:92]cm) only
Shape for sleeves

Next row 12ch, 1dc into 4th ch from hook, 1dc into each of rem 8ch, then work 1dc into each dc to within last dc, using a separate ball of yarn, sl st into last dc of previous row and work 10ch, then fasten off. Return to end of row just worked and work 1dc into last dc, then 1dc into each of the 10ch. Turn. 103[107:113]dc.***
Work 20[20:22] rows in dc.

Shape upper sleeve and shoulder

Next row Sl st over first 6dc, 1hdc into each of next 6dc, 1dc into each of next 25[26:28]dc, work 2dc tog, turn and work on this side only.
Next row Work 2dc tog, 1dc into each of next 6[7:9]dc, 1hdc into each of next 6dc, 1sc into each of next 6dc. Fasten off. Return to rem sts. Leave center 25[27:29]dc free, rejoin yarn to next dc,

3ch, work 2dc tog, 1dc into each of next 24[25:26]dc, 1hdc into each of next 6dc. Fasten off.
Next row Skip first 6hdc and 6dc, rejoin yarn to next dc, into each of next 5dc, 1hdc into each of next 6dc, 1dc into each of next 6[7:9]dc, work 2dc tog. Fasten off.

Waistband

With RS facing, using No. 2 (2¾mm) needles and A pick up and K 102[106:112] sts along foundation ch. Work 2¼in (6cm) in K1 tbl, P1 ribbing. Bind off in ribbing.

Sizes 38[40:42]in (97[102:107]cm) only
Shape armholes

Next row Sl st over first 6dc, 3ch, 1dc into each dc to within last 5dc, turn. 87[91:97]dc.***
Work 24[26:26] rows in dc.

Shape shoulders

Next row Sl st over first 5dc, 1hdc into each of next 5dc, 1dc into each of next 16[17:19]dc, work 2dc tog, turn and work on this side only.
Next row Work 2dc tog, 1dc into each of next 3dc, 1hdc into each of next 4[4:5]dc, 1hdc into each of next 4[4:5]dc. Fasten off.
Return to rem sts. Leave center 31[33:35]dc free, rejoin yarn to next dc, 3ch, work 2dc tog, 1dc into each of next 15[16:18]dc, 1hdc into each of next 5dc. Fasten off.
Next row Skip first 5hdc and 4[5:5]dc, rejoin yarn to next dc, 1sc into each of next 4[4:5]dc, 1hdc into each of next 4[4:5]dc, 1dc into each of next 3dc, work 2dc tog. Fasten off.

Waistband

With RS facing, using No. 2 (2¾mm) needles and A, pick up and K 116[120: 126] sts along foundation ch. Work 2¼in (6cm) K1 tbl, P1 ribbing. Bind off in ribbing.

Front

Work as for back to **. Work 2 rows dc. Now work diamonds, joining on another ball of A for second half of work and, when changing colors. Always change to next color on last loop of preceding st and make 1ch with new color—this brings new color into position for this row. Take yarn not in use across WS of work and catch strand in with each st worked.
1st row With A, 3ch, 1dc into each of next 40[42:45:47:49:52]dc, with B, 1dc into next dc, join on another ball of A and work 1dc into each dc to end. Turn.

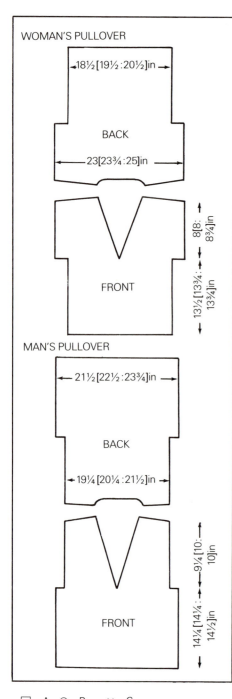

WOMAN'S PULLOVER

←18½[19½:20½]in→

BACK

←23[23¾:25]in→

8[8: 8¾]in

FRONT

13½[13¾: 13¾]in

MAN'S PULLOVER

←21½[22½:23¾]in→

BACK

←19¼[20¼:21½]in→

9¼[10: 10]in

FRONT

14¼[14¼: 14½]in

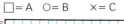
John Hutchinson

□ = A   ○ = B   × = C

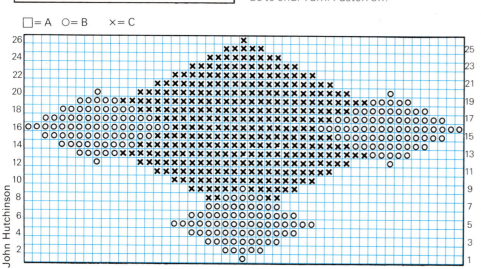

2nd row With A, 3ch, 1dc into each of next 38[40:43:45:47:50]dc, with B, 1dc into each of next 5dc, with A, 1dc into each dc to end. Turn.

Cont in patt as set, foll chart, and on 8th row join on C for center diamond and cut off B on 9th row after the first small diamond has been completed. On 12th row divide B into two separate balls and join one ball for each small diamond at each side. Cont working from chart until 26th row has been completed. Cut off B and C and cont with A only. Work as back to ***.

Sizes 32[34:36]in (83[87:92]cm) only
Divide for neck
Next row 3ch, 1dc into each of next 49[51:54]dc, work 2dc tog, turn and work on this side only.
Next row 3ch, work 2dc tog, 1dc into each dc to end. Turn.
Next row Work to within last 2dc, work 2dc tog. Turn.
Rep last 2 rows until 37[38:40]dc rem. Work 5[4:5] rows without shaping, so ending at sleeve edge.
Shape shoulder
Next row Sl st over next 6dc, 1hdc into each of next 6dc, 1dc into each dc to end. Turn.
Next row 3ch, 1dc into each of next 6[7:9]dc, 1hdc into each of next 6dc, 1sc into each of next 6dc. Fasten off.
Rejoin yarn to next dc at center front.
Next row 3ch, 1dc into each dc to end. Turn.
Next row Work to within last 2dc, work 2dc tog. Turn.
Next row 3ch, work 2dc tog, 1dc into each dc to end. Turn.
Rep last 2 rows until 37[38:40]dc rem. Work 5[4:5] rows without shaping, so ending at neck edge.
Shape shoulder
Next row Work to within last 12dc, 1hdc into each of next 6dc. Fasten off.
Next row Skip first 6hdc and 6dc, rejoin yarn to next dc, 1sc into each of next 5dc, 1hdc into each of next 6dc, 1dc into each dc to end. Turn. Fasten off.

Work waistband as for back.
Sizes [40:42]in (97[102:107]cm) only
Divide for neck
Next row 3ch, 1dc into each of next 41[43:46]dc, work 2dc tog, turn and work on this side only.
Next row 3ch, work 2dc tog, 1dc into each dc to end. Turn.
Next row Work to within last 2dc, work 2dc tog. Turn.
Rep last 2 rows until 26[27:29]dc rem. Work 6[7:6] rows without shaping, so ending at armhole edge.
Shape shoulder
Next row Sl st over first 5dc, 1hdc into each of next 5dc, 1dc into each dc to end. Turn.
Next row 3ch, 1dc into each of next 3dc, 1hdc into each of next 4[4:5]dc, 1sc into each of next 4[4:5]dc. Fasten off.
Rejoin yarn to next dc at center front.
Next row 3ch, 1dc into each dc to end. Turn.
Next row Work to within last 2dc, work 2dc tog. Turn.
Next row 3ch, work 2dc tog, 1dc into each dc to end. Turn.
Rep last 2 rows until 26[27:29]dc rem. Work 6[7:6] rows without shaping, so ending at neck edge.
Shape shoulder
Next row Work to within last 10dc, 1hdc into each of next 5dc. Fasten off.
Next row Skip first 5hdc and 4[5:5]dc, rejoin yarn to next dc, 1sc into each of next 4[4:5]dc, 1hdc into each of next 4[4:5]dc, 1dc into each of next 4dc. Fasten off. Work waistband as for back.
To finish
Using B, outline diamonds in stem stitch as shown on page 93. Press (omitting ribbing) or block, according to yarn used. Join right shoulder seam.
Neck border
With RS facing, using No. 2 (2¾mm) needles and A, pick up and K 66[66:72: 78:82:82] sts along left front neck, pick up and K 1 st from base of V and mark this st with a colored thread, pick up and K 66[66:72:78:82:82] sts along right front neck and 49[51:53:55:57:59] sts along back neck.
Next row *K1 tbl, P1, rep from * to end. Work 6 rows in K1 tbl, P1 ribbing, dec 1 st at each side of marked st on every row and K tbl marked st on RS and P on WS. Bind off in ribbing.
Join left shoulder and neck border seam.
Sizes 32[34:36]in (83[87:92]cm) only
Sleeve borders (alike)
With RS facing, using No. 2 (2¾mm) needles and A, pick up and K 106[106: 116] sts evenly along sleeve edge. Work 7 rows in K1 tbl, P1 ribbing. Bind off in ribbing.
Sizes 38[40:42]in (97[102:107]cm):
Using size E (3.50mm) hook and A, work 2 rows of sc along armhole edge. Fasten off.
All sizes: Join side seams. Press seams on wrong side.

94

Floral fantasy

A big bunch of flowers is the inspiration for this beautiful sweater. And following a chart makes it easier to make than you might think.

1 ball in each of 8 contrasting colors (see chart)
Size E (3.50mm) crochet hook
1 pair No. 2 (3mm) knitting needles

Sizes

To fit 34[36:38]in (87[92:97]cm) bust.
Length, 21in (54cm).
Sleeve seam, 17½[17¾:18]in (44[45:46]cm).
Note: Directions for larger sizes are in brackets [ ]; if there is only one set of figures it applies to all sizes.

Materials

7[8:8]×2oz (50g) balls of a sport yarn in main color (A)

Gauge

20hdc and 16 rows to 4in (10cm) worked with size E (3.50mm) hook.
20 sc and 24 rows to 4in (10cm) worked with size E (3.50mm) hook.

Front

Using size E (3.50mm) hook and A, make 93[97:101]ch.
Base row 1sc into 2nd ch from hook, 1sc into each ch to end. Turn. 93[97:101]sc.
Next row 1ch to count as first sc, 1sc into each sc to end. Turn.
Cont in sc, working in patt from chart until the 106th row has been worked, then work 2 rows in A. Fasten off.

Waistband

Using No. 2 (3mm) needles, with RS facing and A, pick up and K 93[97:101] sts evenly along foundation edge.
1st ribbing row K1, (P1, K1) to end.
2nd ribbing row P1, (K1, P1) to end.
Rep these 2 rows for 2in (5cm). Bind off loosely in ribbing.

Neckband

Using No. 2 (3mm) needles, with RS facing and A, pick up and K 135[139:143] sts evenly along top edge. Work 2 ribbing rows of waistband for ¾in (2cm). Bind off in ribbing.

Back

Using size E (3.50mm) hook and A, make 94[98:102] ch.
Base row 1hdc into 3rd ch from hook, 1hdc into each ch to end. Turn. 93[97:101]hdc.
Next row 2ch to count as first hdc, 1hdc into each hdc to end. Turn. Cont in hdc until work measures the same as front. Fasten off.

Waistband

Work as for front waistband.

Neckband

Work as for front neckband.

Sleeves

Using size E (3.50mm) hook and A, make 63[67:71] ch. Work base row as for back, then cont in hdc inc 1 hdc at each end of 7th and every foll 6th row until there are 80[84:88] hdc. Cont straight until work measures 15½[15¾:16]in (39[40:41]cm). Fasten off.

Cuff

Using No. 2 (3mm) needles and A, pick up and K 53[55:59] sts evenly along foundation edge. Rib 2 rib rows for 2in (5cm). Bind off loosely in ribbing.

To finish

Press or block, according to yarn used. Join shoulder seams, leaving 9in (23cm) open at center for neck. Sew sleeves to back and front, then join side and sleeve seams.

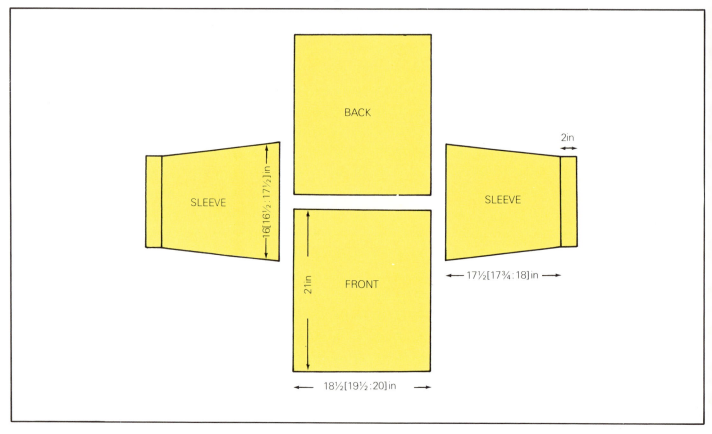

100

90

80

70

60

50

40

30

20

10

3rd 2nd 1st

1st 2nd 3rd

KEY ☐ mauve ❮ green ● yellow ❙ beige ― brown ✖ red ▽ rose ○ pink ╱ peach ● cream

KNITTING

Triple ripple

Three soft shades ripple through this bloused cardigan to wear with your most feminine clothes.

Sizes To fit 32-34[36-38]in (83-87[92-97]cm) bust.
Length, 22[23]in (56[58]cm).
Sleeve seam, 18in (46cm).
Note Directions for larger size are in brackets []; where there is only one set of figures it applies to both sizes.

Materials
8oz (200g) of a lightweight mohair in main color (A)
6oz (150g) in each of 2 contrasting colors (B and C)
1 pair each Nos. 3 and 5 (3¼ and 4mm) knitting needles
7 buttons

Gauge
22 sts and 30 rows to 4in (10cm) pattern on No. 5 (4mm) needles.

Back
Using No. 3 (3¼mm) needles and A, cast on 96[108] sts; work K1, P1 ribbing for 3in (7.5cm).
Inc row Rib 10, pick up horizontal loop lying between needles and work into back of it—called make 1 or M1—, *rib 7[8], M1, rep from * to last 9[10] sts, rib to end. 108[120] sts.
Change to No. 5 (4mm) needles. Joining on colors as required, beg patt.
1st row (RS) With A, K to end.
2nd row With A, P to end.
3rd row With A, *(K2 tog tbl) twice, (yo, K1) 4 times, (K2 tog tbl) twice, rep from * to end.
4th row With B, K to end.
5th-7th rows As 1st-3rd rows but use B instead of A.
8th row With C, K to end.
9th-11th rows As 1st-3rd rows but use C instead of A.
12th row With A, K to end.
These 12 rows form patt.
Cont in patt until work measures 13in (33cm); end with a WS row. Place a marker at each end of last row. Cont in patt until work measures 22[23]in (56[58]cm); end with a WS row.
Shape shoulders
Bind off 10[11] sts at beg of next 6 rows. Cut off yarn and leave rem 48[54] sts on a holder.

Left front
**Using No. 3 (3¼mm) needles and A, cast on 48[54]sts and work in K1, P1 ribbing for 3in (7.5cm).
Inc row Rib 6[10], M1, *rib 6[7], M1, rep from * to last 6[9] sts, rib to end. 55[60] sts. Change to No. 5 (4mm) needles. Joining on colors as required, beg patt.**
1st size only
1st row (RS) With A, K to end.
2nd row With A, P to end.
3rd row With A, *(K2 tog tbl) twice, (yo, K1) 4 times, (K2 tog tbl) twice, rep fom * to last 7 sts, (K2 tog tbl) twice, (yo, K1) twice, K1.
4th row With B, K to end.
5th-7th rows As 1st-3rd rows but use B instead of A.
8th row With C, K to end.
9th-11th rows As 1st-3rd rows but use C instead of A.
12th row With A, K to end.
These 12 rows form patt.
2nd size only
1st row (RS) With A, K to end.
2nd row With A, P to end.
3rd row With A, *(K2 tog tbl) twice, (yo, K1) 4 times, (K2 tog tbl) twice, rep from * to end.
4th row With B, K to end.
5th-7th rows As 1st-3rd rows but use B instead of A.
8th row With C, K to end.
9th-11th rows As 1st-3rd rows but use C instead of A.
12th row With A, K to end.
These 12 rows form patt.
Both sizes
Cont in patt until work measures 13in (33cm); end with a WS row. Place a marker at end of last row. Cont in patt until work measures 18[19]in (46[48]cm); end with a WS row.
Shape neck
Next row Patt to last 12 sts, turn and leave these 12 sts on a safety pin. Keeping patt correct, dec one st at neck edge on every foll alternate row until 30[35] sts rem. Cont straight until front is same length as back to shoulders; end at side edge.

Shape shoulder
Bind off 10[11] sts at beg of next and foll alternate row. Work 1 row. Bind off.

Right front
Work as for left front from ** to **.
1st size only
1st row (RS) With A, K to end.
2nd row With A, P to end.
3rd row With A, K1, (K1, yo) twice, (K2 tog tbl) twice, *(K2 tog tbl) twice, (yo, K1) 4 times, (K2 tog tbl) twice, rep from * to end.
4th row With B, K to end.
5th-7th rows As 1st-3rd rows but use B instead of A.
8th row With C, K to end.
9th-11th rows As 1st-3rd rows but use C instead of A.
12th row With A, K to end.
These 12 rows form patt.
2nd size only
1st row (RS) With A, K to end.
2nd row With A, P to end.
3rd row With A, *(K2 tog tbl) twice, (yo, K1) 4 times, (K2 tog tbl) twice, rep from * to end.
4th row With B, K to end.
5th-7th rows As 1st-3rd rows but use B instead of A.
8th row With C, K to end.
9th-11th rows As 1st-3rd rows but use C instead of A.
12th row With A, K to end.
These 12 rows form patt.
Both sizes
Complete to match left front reversing shapings and mark beg of row instead of end.

Sleeves
Using No. 3 (3¼mm) needles and A, cast on 46[48] sts and work in K1, P1 ribbing for 3in (7.5cm).
Inc row *Rib 1, M1, rep from * to last st, rib 1. 91[95] sts.
Next row P5[11], inc in next st, (P4 [2], inc in next st) 16[24] times, P5 [11]. 108[120] sts.
Cont in patt as for back until work measures 18in (46cm); end with a WS row. Bind off.

Neck border

Join shoulder seams. With RS facing using No. 3 (3¼mm) needles and A, K 12 sts from right front, pick up and K 30[32] sts up right side of neck, K the sts from holder dec one st at center, pick up and K 30[32] sts down left side of neck, then K 12 sts from left front. 131[141] sts.

Next row P1, (K1, P1) to end.
Next row K1, (P1, K1) to end.

Rep these 2 rows for 1in (2.5cm). Bind off in ribbing.

Button border Using No. 3 (3¼mm) needles and A, cast on 7 sts.
1st rib row (RS) K2, (P1, K1) twice, K1.
2nd rib row (K1, P1) 3 times, K1.
Rep these 2 rows until border, slightly stretched, fits up left front to top of neck border. Bind off in ribbing.

Mark 7 button positions on this border, the first ½in (1cm) from cast-on edge, the last ½in (1cm) from bound-off edge and the others evenly spaced between.

Buttonhole border Work as for button border but make buttonholes to correspond with markers as foll:
Buttonhole row (RS) Rib 3, yo, P2 tog, rib 2.

To finish

Do not press. Set in sleeves between markers, then join side and sleeve seams. Sew on the borders and buttons.

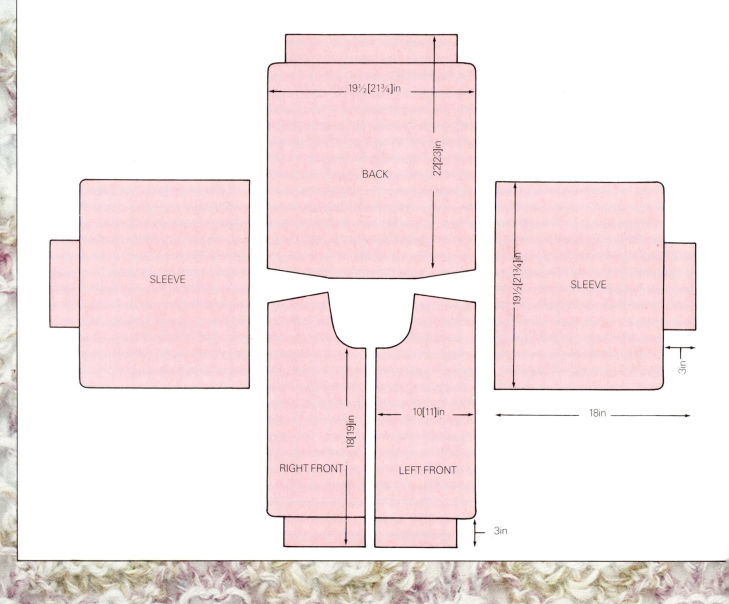

BACK — 19½[21¾]in — 22[23]in

SLEEVE — 19½[21¾]in — 18in — 3in

SLEEVE — 3in

RIGHT FRONT — 18[19]in

LEFT FRONT — 10[11]in — 3in

EXTRA SPECIAL KNITTING

Work-of-art vest

Color and texture cleverly combined create a vest that's a real masterpiece.

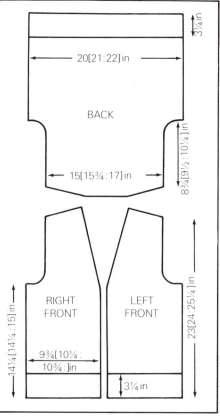

Sizes
To fit 38[40:42]in (97[102:107]cm) chest.
Length to shoulder, 23[24:25¼]in (58[61:64]cm).

Note: Directions for the larger sizes are in brackets []; if there is only one set of figures it applies to all sizes.

Materials
6oz (150g) of a knitting worsted in main color (A)
2[2:4]oz (50[50:100]g) in contrasting color (B)
2oz (50g) in contrasting color (C)
2oz (50g) in contrasting color (D)
4oz (80g) of a medium-weight bouclé in contrasting color (E)
4oz (80g) of bouclé in contrasting color (F)
1 pair each Nos. 3 and 5 (3¼ and 4mm) knitting needles
6 buttons

Gauge
22 sts and 28 rows to 4in (10cm) in stockinette st on No. 5 (4mm) needles and knitting worsted.

Back
Using No. 5 (4mm) needles and A, cast on 110[114:120] sts. Work 3¼in (8cm) K1, P1 ribbing, inc one st at end of last row on 3rd size only. 110[114:121] sts. Beg with a K row, work 4 rows stockinette st. Join in B. Beg patt.
1st row K3[5:0], *K2, pick up loop lying between needles and K tbl—called make 1, or "M1"—K6, sl 1, K2 tog, psso, K6, M1, rep from * to last 5[7:2] sts, K5[7:2].
2nd row P to end.
These 2 rows form patt. Rep them throughout, working in stripe sequence of 2 more rows B, 4 rows each of B, C, E, A and F, 8 rows B, 4 rows each of E, D, F, E, F and A. Cont in patt until work measures 14¼[14½:15]in (36[37:38]cm); end with a WS row.

Shape armholes
Bind off 7 sts at beg of next 2 rows. Dec one st at each end of next and foll 6 alternate rows. 82[86:93] sts. Cont straight until armholes measure 8¾[9½: 10¼]in (22[24:26]cm); end with a WS row.

Shape shoulders
Bind off 8[9:9] sts at beg of next 4 rows and 9[8:10] sts at beg of foll 2 rows. Bind off rem 32[34:37] sts.

Right front
Using No. 5 (4mm) needles and A, cast on 52[56:58] sts. Work 3¼in (8cm) K1, P1 ribbing, inc one st at end of last row. 53[57:59] sts. Beg with a K row, work 4 rows stockinette st. Join in B. Beg patt.
1st row K0[2:3], *K2, M1, K6, sl 1, K2 tog, psso, K6, M1, rep from * to last 2[4:5] sts, K2[4:5].
2nd row P to end.
Cont in patt and stripe sequence as for back until front matches back to underarms; end with a RS row.

Shape armhole and front edge
Bind off 7 sts at beg of next row. Dec one st at armhole edge on next and 6 foll alternate rows, **at same time** dec one st at front edge on next and every foll 3rd row until 25[26:28] sts rem. Cont straight until front matches back to shoulders; end at armhole edge.

Shape shoulder
Bind off 8[9:9] sts at beg of next and foll alternate row. Work 1 row. Bind off rem 9[8:10] sts.

Left front
Work as for right front, reversing shaping.

Front band
Join shoulder seams. Using No. 3 (3¼mm) needles and A, cast on 10 sts. Work ⅜in (1cm) K1, P1 ribbing.
Next row (buttonhole row) Rib 4, bind off 2 sts, rib to end.
Next row Rib to end, casting on 2 sts over those bound off in previous row. Cont in ribbing, making 5 more buttonholes 2¼in (6cm) apart, measured from base of previous buttonhole, until band, when slightly stretched, fits up left front, around back neck and down right front. Bind off in ribbing.

Armbands
Using No. 3 (3¼mm) needles, A and with RS facing, pick up and K100[104:108] sts around armhole. Work 1¼in (3cm) K1, P1 ribbing. Cast off loosely in ribbing.

To finish
Block the work. Join side seams. Sew on front band and buttons.

These charming sunsuits have buttons at the neck and waist so that they are easy to slip on and off. Elasticized bloomers are big enough to go over diapers and the girl's version is completed with a bonnet.

Measurements

The suit can be made in two sizes, to fit a 9- to 18-month-old baby or an 18-month to 2-year-old toddler.

Materials

Panties
$\frac{3}{4}$yd (.6m) of 36in (90cm)-wide fabric
$2\frac{1}{4}$yd (2m) narrow elastic
$1\frac{5}{8}$yd (1.2m) bias binding

Top
$\frac{1}{2}$yd (.4m) of 36in (90cm)-wide fabric
Scrap of contrasting fabric
$\frac{7}{8}$yd (75cm) of narrow eyelet edging (optional)
Four buttons

Bonnet
$\frac{1}{4}$yd (.2m) of 36in (90cm)-wide fabric
$\frac{5}{8}$yd (.5m) of wide eyelet edging
$\frac{7}{8}$yd (.7m) of $\frac{3}{8}$in (1cm)-wide ribbon
Matching thread for all garments

Suggested fabrics

Cotton, gingham, seersucker or, for the top and panties, terrycloth.
Note Measurements are given for the smaller size, with measurements for the larger size in brackets. If only one figure is given, it applies to both sizes.

Panties

1 Make a paper pattern, based on a rectangle 11[12]in (28[30]cm) by $22\frac{1}{2}$[24]in (57[61]cm). Following measurement diagram, draw pattern for side pieces. Cut out two pieces of fabric this size.

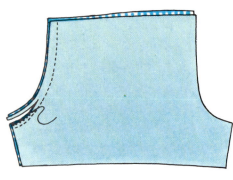

2 Join center back and center front seams. Trim seam allowances and finish together.

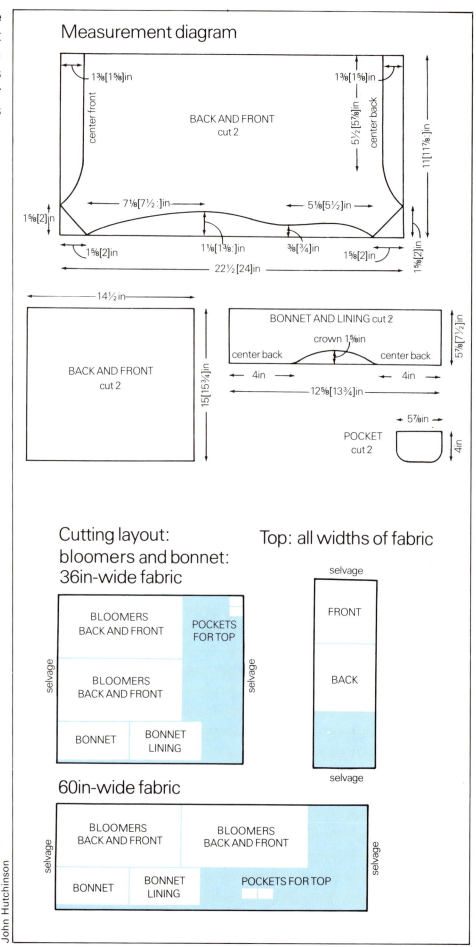

John Hutchinson

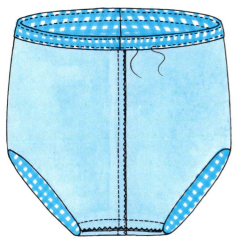

3 Turn under ¼in (6mm) around upper edge. Turn under another ⅝in (1.5cm); pin and baste in place. Stitch around waist, close to each foldline, to form a casing for the elastic, leaving a short opening close to center front seam.

4 Join crotch seam. Trim seam allowances and finish raw edges together.

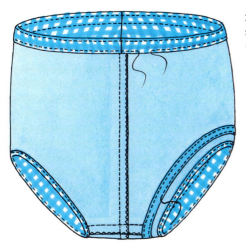

5 Make a ¼in (6mm) double hem around each leg opening. For the elastic casing, pin, baste and stitch bias binding around leg, positioning it ⅝in (1.5cm) from finished edge. Leave opening for elastic.

6 Measure the baby's waist and upper leg. Cut three pieces of elastic, adding 6in (15cm) to each measurement. Thread elastic through casing and knot ends temporarily. Try on for fit. Trim ends of elastic, sew together securely, and slip stitch openings to close.

Top

1 Cut two rectangles of fabric 14½ × 15[15¾]in (37 × 38[40]cm). From same fabric, make a tube 10in (25cm) long and cut into four equal pieces for button loops.

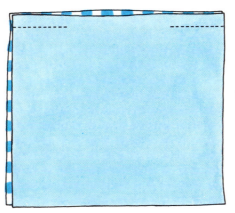

2 Pin front to back and pin, baste and stitch shoulder seams 2in (5cm) from sleeve edge. Press seams open.

3 Turn under and stitch ¼in (6mm) along shoulder seam allowances and across neck edges to finish.

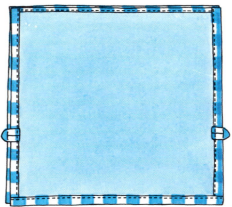

4 Turn under and pin a ⅜in (1cm) - wide double hem down side edges and across

lower edge of top. Position a tube loop on each side of front section 6in (15cm) down from shoulder seams. Tuck the raw ends of the tube loop into the hem and fold the loop out. Baste around hem and stitch close to inner edge of hem, catching loops in place at the same time.

5 Turn under and pin a ⅜in (1cm) - wide hem across neck edge. Pin tube loops to back section, positioning each one 2in (5cm) in from end of seam stitching. Tuck raw ends into hem. Baste and stitch hem across neck edges, catching loops in place, and continuing stitching at each side of neck so that the shoulder seams are topstitched.

6 Sew buttons to front section at neck edge and to back section at sides, positioning buttons to take in fullness.

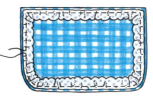

7 Cut two pocket pieces, following the measurement diagram, using a contrasting fabric. For girl's version, run a gathering thread through narrow eyelet edging. Pin to right side of one pocket section around all edges, distributing fullness and drawing up thread so ends meet. Join ends of eyelet lace.

Pin second pocket section over first, right sides together, so that raw edges of eyelet lace are sandwiched. Baste

Victor Yuan

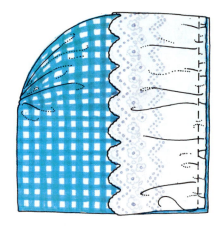

3 Run a line of gathering through wide eyelet edging and pin to right side of one bonnet section, drawing up threads and distributing fullness evenly. Place second bonnet section over first, right sides together and raw edges matching. Pin, baste and stitch around front of bonnet, enclosing raw edges of eyelet.

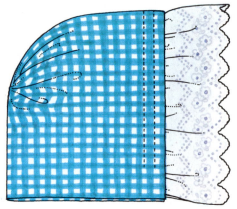

4 Turn bonnet right side out. Stitch two casing lines, $\frac{3}{8}$in (1cm) apart, $\frac{3}{8}$in (1cm) from front edge of bonnet, finishing stitches 2in (5cm) from raw edges at short sides of bonnet. Make a slit inside the bonnet at each end of the casing. Overcast edges of slits to finish.

and stitch the pocket pieces together, leaving a 1in (2.5cm)-long opening in the lower edge.
8 For boy's version, stitch the two sections together as described for girl's pocket, omitting eyelet.

Bonnet

1 Cut out two rectangles of fabric, 6[7$\frac{1}{2}$]in (15[19]cm) × 12$\frac{5}{8}$[13$\frac{3}{4}$]in (32[35]cm), shaping one long edge of each as shown in measurement diagram.

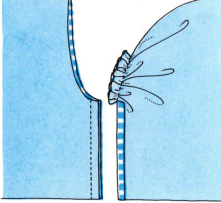

9 Turn pocket right side out and slip stitch opening to close. On girl's version, make sure that eyelet is caught in.
10 Topstitch pocket to center front of top.

2 Pin, baste and stitch center back seam along straight section of each bonnet piece. Run a line of gathering along the curved crown edge of each piece and draw up tightly. Tie off threads. Trim raw edges of gathered section and finish. Press seam open along straight section.

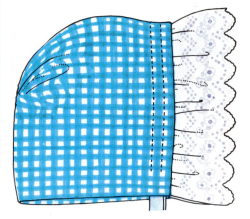

5 Turn in open edges around lower edge of bonnet and slip stitch to close.
6 Thread ribbon through casing and gather up bonnet to fit.

Victor Yuan

Sewing

Buckled and tied

Accessories can add a bit of snap to your wardrobe but can be very expensive to buy. Here are some ideas for making your own dashing belts and scarves for a song.

David Bradfield

Soft belt

Measurements
The belt is designed to fit standard waists, from 25 to 27½in (64 to 70cm).

Materials
⅜yd (.3m) of 36in (90cm)-wide imitation suede
2in (5cm)-wide buckle; thread

Suggested fabrics
The belt should be made from suede or imitation suede or a suitably-stiffened woven fabric.

1 Cut a piece of fabric 10in (25cm) by the waist measurement, plus 1½in (4cm) for seams and 7in (18cm) for overlap.

2 Fold fabric in half down its length, right sides together, and machine stitch long raw edges, stitching diagonally across one short edge as shown.
3 Trim seam allowance, clip corners and turn belt right side out.

4 On the right side, topstitch ¼in (5mm) from stitched and folded edges, and across straight end.

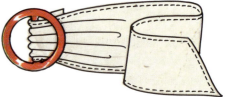

5 Fold 1½in (4cm) of straight end over buckle bar and sew raw edges to wrong side of belt.

David Bradfield

Terry Evans

108

Cummerbund

Measurements

The cummerbund can be made to fit a waist up to 34in (86cm) around (from 36in [90cm] fabric) up to 42½in (108cm) (from 45in [115cm] wide fabric).

Materials

⅝yd (.6m) of 36/45in (90/115cm)-wide satin
⅜yd (.3m) of 36/45in (90/115cm)-wide lining
⅜yd (.3m) of 36in (90cm)-wide interfacing (double for larger waist)
12in (30cm) matching seam binding
6 hooks and eyes; paper for pattern

1 Cut belt to measurements given on measurement diagram. Make a paper pattern and mark pleat lines on it. Pin pattern to satin fabric and transfer markings with lines of basting. Cut a lining piece 6¾in (17cm) wide and same length as cummerbund, and an interfacing piece the same size as lining. Cut two strips of seam binding 6¾in (17cm) long.

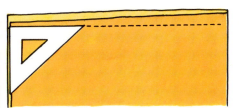

2 Fold and baste all pleats on the satin fabric. Baste interfacing to wrong side of lining.
3 With right sides together, baste interfaced lining to pleated section. Stitch along both edges and one short edge. Grade the seam allowances, clip corners and turn cummerbund right side

out. Prick stitch (tiny, spaced running stitches) around stitched edges to hold shape. Press.
4 At finished end, sew a piece of binding to wrong side, turning under both ends of binding and matching to finished edges of cummerbund. Sew 6 hooks evenly down strip.

5 At unfinished end, turn in ⅝in (1.5cm) and pin, baste and stitch the other piece of binding to the right side of the cummerbund. Sew eyes down binding to match hooks.
6 Remove all basting and press lightly from wrong side.

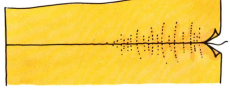

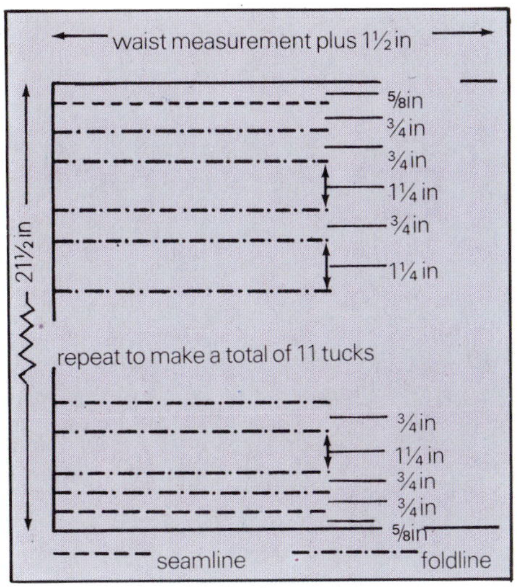

```
←——— waist measurement plus 1½in ———→
                                    ⅝in
                                    ¾in
                                    ¾in
                                    1¼in
                                    ¾in
21½in                               1¼in

    repeat to make a total of 11 tucks

                                    ¾in
                                    1¼in
                                    ¾in
                                    ¾in
                                    ⅝in
- - - - seamline    - · - · - foldline
```

Fringed scarf

Measurements

Finished scarf measures 13½ × 60in (34×152cm).

Materials

⅜yd (.4m) of 60in (152cm)-wide, loosely woven fabric
Fine sewing thread to match

1 Find straight grain of fabric by pulling a thread, and straighten fabric if necessary (see Technique Tip). Trim fabric, if necessary, to 13½in (34cm), and remove selvages.
2 With machine set to a short, narrow zig-zag stitch and following the grain of the fabric, stitch all around scarf, ⅜in (1cm) from the long edges and 1¼in (3cm) from the short edges.

3 From one edge at a time, unravel threads as far as line of stitching.

Square scarf

Measurements

The finished scarf measures 31in (79cm) square.

Materials

1yd (.9m) of 36in (90cm)-wide fabric
Matching thread

Suggested fabrics

Silk, silk-like synthetics, lightweight wools or wool blends.
1 Find straight grain of fabric and straighten if necessary (see Technique Tip).
Cut out a 31½in (80cm) square.
2 Machine stitch ¼in (5mm) in from all edges. Trim fabric close to stitching.

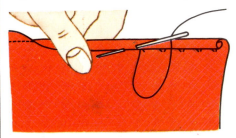

3 Dampen first finger and thumb of left hand and, with the wrong side uppermost, roll the edge of the scarf in short even lengths, slip stitching it in place with the right hand.
4 Press on wrong side, but do not press rolled edge.

Technique tips

Straightening fabric

The wool scarf and silk square must be cut on the straight grain of the fabric.

If the weft threads do not run straight across the fabric (check with a right-triangle placed with one edge along a selvage) dampen the fabric slightly and stretch it diagonally to pull the threads straight. If the threads are still not straight, wrap fabric in a damp towel, leave it overnight, and stretch again. The threads should run across the fabric at right angles to the selvage.

Cutting on the straight grain

To ensure that the scarves are cut on the straight grain (on even-weave fabrics) you will need to pull a thread.

Clip into the selvage and find a weft thread (one that runs from selvage to selvage). When you pull the thread, the fabric will pucker but can easily be smoothed again with the fingers. As you draw out the thread, a line will form across the fabric; use as a cutting line.
If you are using a crepe, twill or any other fabric from which a thread cannot be pulled, straighten the fabric and then use a right triangle to mark across the fabric, aligning it with a selvage.

Needlework EXTRA

Smart settings

Clamshell patchwork is based on curved shapes and is therefore tricky to work. Here it is used in different ways to decorate placemats and matching napkins.

Materials
 Eight 16½in (42cm)-square plain
  linen napkins
 ¾yd (.7m) of 36in (90cm)-wide
  plain cotton fabric for backing
 ⅝yd (.5m) of 36in (90cm)-wide
  cotton fabric in three different
  prints
 Thick cardboard for templates
 Tracing paper; heavy paper
 Sharp craft knife
 5½yd (5m) of filler cord
 5½yd (5m) of ½in (1.2cm)-wide bias
  binding in a color contrasting with
  napkins
 Matching thread

Note Because of the curves involved, it is not advisable to draw your own template. There is a trace pattern for a template on page 112, or buy a 3in (7.5cm) template and matching window template.

Preparing the patches

1 Trace the two templates: a window template for cutting out fabric patches (following the dotted and solid lines) and a plain template for cutting out paper patterns (following only the solid line).
2 Draw the smaller (plain) template on thick cardboard and cut out accurately, using a sharp craft knife.
3 Mark both template outlines, the smaller plain template inside the larger window outline, on the cardboard. Cut out around the outer line accurately, using a sharp craft knife. Then cut around the inner marked line and discard the center piece, making a window.

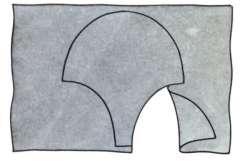

4 Place the smaller template on the heavy paper. Draw around accurately and cut

out carefully. Repeat to make about 90 paper patches.

5 Using the window template, draw around and cut out a selection of patches from the three different printed fabrics: position the template on the wrong side of the fabric, aligning the base of the patch with the straight grain of the fabric. This will make it easier to cover the paper templates with the fabric. The window allows you to see which part of the fabric pattern will show.

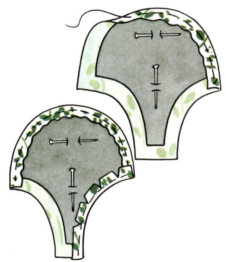

6 Pin a paper template in the center of the wrong side of a fabric patch. Turn the fabric edges over the paper template and baste all edges under. It will be necessary to clip the side curves to produce an accurate shape.
7 Repeat step 6 to cover all the paper patches.

Napkins

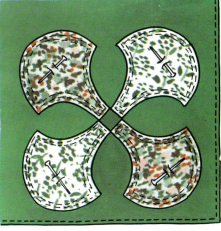

1 Use four clamshell patches for each napkin. Choose the patches and arrange four in the corner of one napkin as shown. The stalks of the four clamshell patches should just touch one another in the center of the design.
2 Pin and baste each patch to the napkin.

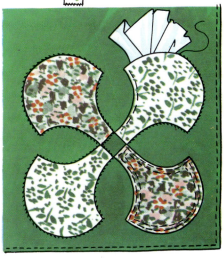

3 With thread that matches the napkin, work small slip stitches around each patch in the direction shown above. Sew the base lines of the stalks first to make a neat square in the center and then sew the side curves. Before sewing each patch along the top curve, remove the basting stitches and carefully ease the paper patch out. Continue to sew, tucking in the overlap to keep the curved shape.
4 When the stitching is complete, press the napkin on the wrong side.
5 Repeat steps 1 to 4 and make three more napkins in the same way.

Terry Evans

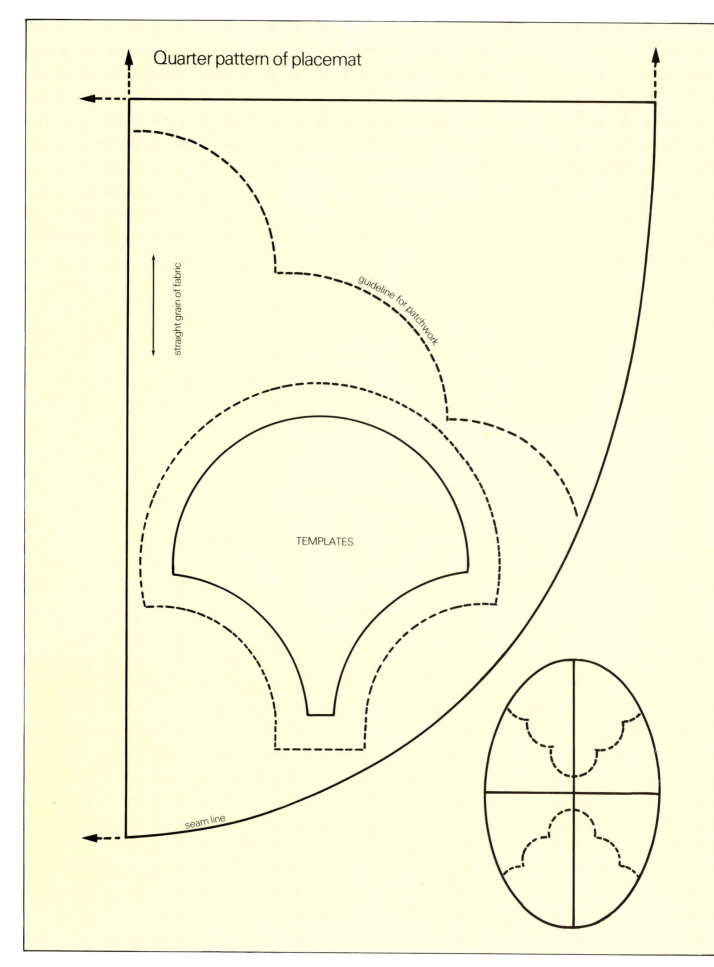

Quarter pattern of placemat

straight grain of fabric

guideline for patchwork

TEMPLATES

seam line

John Hutchinson

Place mats

1 Press one remaining napkin flat.
2 To make the pattern for the placemat, cut a piece of tracing paper 8¼ × 6in (21 × 15cm); fold in half each way, creasing paper well; unfold paper and place one quarter over pattern on opposite page, matching folded lines with center lines. Mark outer curved line and the guideline for the edge of the patchwork, then fold paper into quarters again. Keeping quarters together cut around marked outer line. Unfold pattern.
3 Place pattern on napkin, leaving a border at least ¾in (2cm) wide all around for a seam. Pin pattern in place. Baste around edge to mark seamline on napkin.

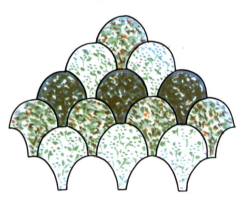

4 Select the patches and arrange colors to make an attractive pattern.

5 Following this arrangement and using white sewing thread, sew patches together by hand, working from the wrong side. Hold the patches flat in the hand and, with each stitch, catch a small amount of fabric (but not the paper patches) from each patch along their common sides.
6 Build up the section of patchwork until you have five rows in a triangular shape as shown. Press flat on the right side.
7 Work a matching patchwork block for the other end of the placemat.

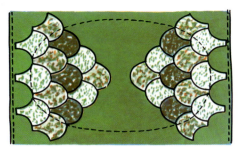

8 Using the tracing paper pattern as a guide for positioning the patchwork, lay each patchwork section over the basted shape of placemat. Pin and baste around patchwork sections.
9 Slip stitch around the top scalloped edges using thread to match the napkin. Remove all basting threads and remove the paper patches.
10 Make sure all seams are flat and place patchwork on mat as before. Press the mat on the wrong side. Baste around the marked seamline of the placemat, anchoring the free edge of the patchwork sections.
11 To make the cording, press the bias strip open, fold it around the filler cord, wrong side together, and stitch along binding as close to cord as possible.

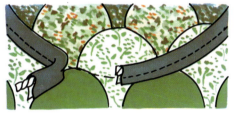

12 Pin covered filler cord around the placemat on the marked seamline with the cord facing the inside of the line. Cut the cord, leaving a ⅝in (1.5cm) overlap.

13 To finish binding, unpick the stitches of the overlapping end for ⅝in (1.5cm). Cut the filler cord, not the bias strip, to butt exactly against the other end of the cord. Fold in ¼in (5mm) of fabric on unpicked bias strip and wrap over the other end of cording to make a neat seam. Slip stitch around the seam in the binding to finish it.
14 Stitch binding in place along seamline. Trim placemat, leaving ⅝in (1.5cm) seam allowance.
15 Using tracing paper pattern, cut out one mat piece from cotton backing fabric, adding ⅝in (1.5cm) seam allowance all around outer edge.

Terry Evans

16 With right sides together, pin and baste the backing fabric to the patchworked oval. Working with the patchwork side up, stitch along the existing stitching line, leaving a 4in (10cm) opening in one long side.
17 Trim excess fabric, leaving ⅜in (1cm) seam allowance, and clip curves.
18 Turn placemat right side out. Turn in opening edges and slip stitch together.
19 Repeat steps 1 to 18 to make three more placemats in the same way.

Homemaker

Toy bag

This sturdy toy bag will hang on the back of a door to provide a handy holdall for the kids. Its bright appliquéd front will cheer up the play-room or bedroom.

Gary Warren

Materials

Piece of unbleached muslin 60 x 20in (152 x 51cm)
Scraps of cotton fabric in solid red, turquoise, yellow, green and lilac
Piece of heavyweight red poplin or sailcloth 20 x 8in (51 x 20cm)
Matching and contrasting sewing threads
2½in (6.5cm) of touch-and-close tape
Tracing paper
Dressmaker's carbon paper
Tissue paper
Bright-colored button

Note ⅝in (1.5cm) seam allowances have been included throughout.

1 Fold muslin in half widthwise. Press and baste along foldline. This will be the base of the bag. Unfold muslin.
2 Trace the motifs from the trace pattern on page 117. Using dressmaker's carbon paper, mark the shapes on the wrong side of the appropriate colored fabrics. Cut out all pieces. Mark the window frames on the right side of the turquoise house piece.

3 Place the two house pieces together, with turquoise on the right side and yellow fabric for windows underneath. Place them on half of the muslin, 2¼in (6cm) from base fold. Pin and baste.

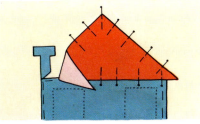

4 Place the roof on top of the house, so that the lower edge overlaps the top of the house. Slip the lower, slanted edge of the chimney under the edge of the roof on the left-hand side of the house. Pin and baste roof and chimney in place.

5 Place the door on the house, centering

it on the base edge. Pin and baste in place. Mark the position of the window on the door. Carefully baste all around the outer edge of the house, very close to the edge.

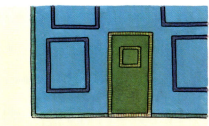

6 Set your sewing machine to satin stitch on medium width and minimum length of stitch. Place a sheet of tissue paper under the muslin and house and satin stitch along all the raw edges. The tissue paper helps to prevent the fabric from puckering as you sew. Begin by stitching the house sides and base edge and the chimney, using turquoise thread to match the house. Sew around the roof using red thread and then around the edge of the door with green thread. Also using green thread, sew around the window of the door. Finally, sew around the outlines of the windows, using dark blue thread, to make the outer frames.
You may find it easier to work if you topstitch the sections in position first.

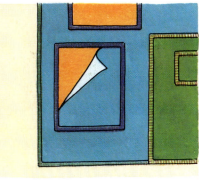

Terry Evans

7 Using sharp pointed scissors, carefully cut away the top layer of fabric from inside the window frames, exposing the yellow fabric underneath. Similarly, cut away the green fabric and then the turquoise fabric from inside the window on the door.

8 Using a contrasting color, satin stitch crossed lines in each of the windows and in the door window. Using a contrasting color, satin stitch a line on the door to represent the mail slot.

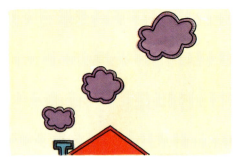

9 Place the smoke clouds in a row, one above the chimney and the next two slightly to the right, graduating in size, as shown. Sew in place, as for the house.
10 Remove the tissue paper and press the appliquéd area on the wrong side.
11 Sew the button to the door, centering it under the mail slot.

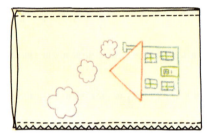

12 Fold muslin in half, right sides facing. Pin, baste and sew side seams. Finish raw edges of seams with zig-zag stitch.
13 Fold over a double ⅜in (1cm)-wide hem all around the top edge. Pin, baste and topstitch around top edge. ·
14 Cut red fabric in half to make two handles, each 20×4in (51×10cm).

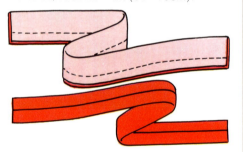

15 Fold each handle in half lengthwise; pin, baste and sew long sides. Turn handles right side out. Press handles flat, with seam centered on wrong side.

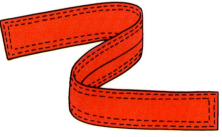

16 Tuck raw edges on each short end of each handle inside; pin and baste. Using

a contrasting thread, topstitch around each handle close to the outer edge. Topstitch, again, about ¼in (5mm) inside first line of stitching.

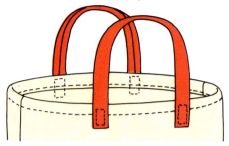

17 Pin and baste handles to the right side of the top edge of each side of bag,

positioning outer edges 5in (13cm) in from side edges of bag, with the ends overlapping top edge for 1½in (4cm). Sew each handle in place at each end over existing stitching lines, as shown.

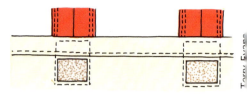

18 Cut touch-and-close tape in half. Pin and baste half of each piece inside the bag, behind the ends of the hands. Pin and baste the other halves of fastening tape behind opposite handle ends. Topstitch

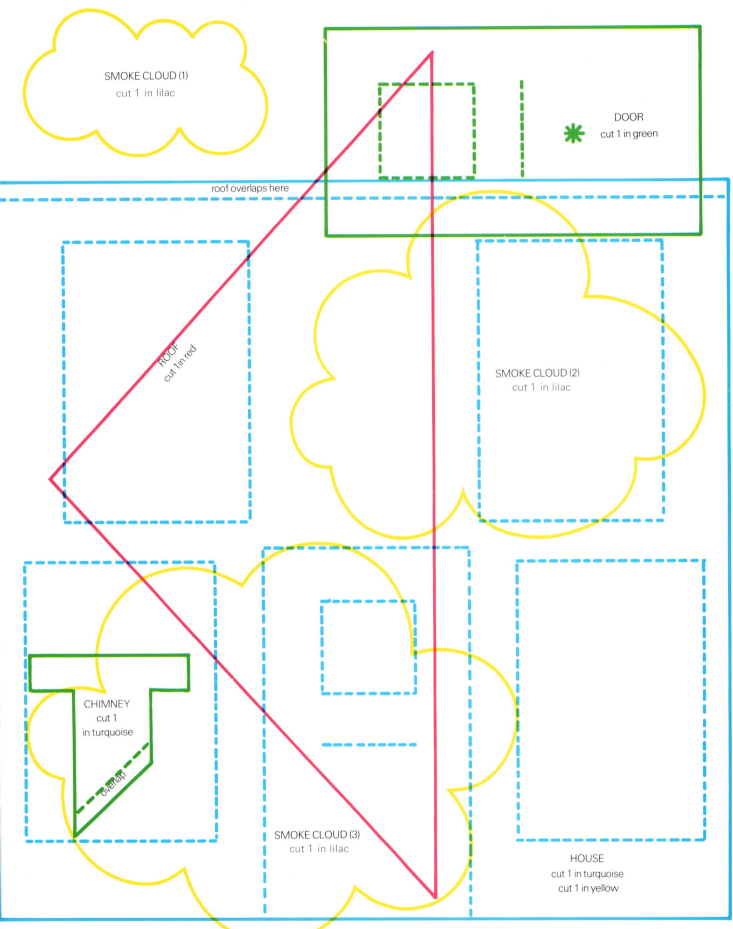

SMOKE CLOUD (1)
cut 1 in lilac

DOOR
cut 1 in green

roof overlaps here

ROOF
cut 1 in red

SMOKE CLOUD (2)
cut 1 in lilac

CHIMNEY
cut 1
in turquoise

overlap

SMOKE CLOUD (3)
cut 1 in lilac

HOUSE
cut 1 in turquoise
cut 1 in yellow

John Hutchinson

Roman style

Roman shades combine the best features of curtains and ordinary window shades—soft folds and classic simplicity.

Materials
> Heavy cotton fabric and lining (see below for amounts)
> 1in (2.5cm)-wide tape with rings for Roman shades
> Nylon cord; cleat
> Picture ring screws
> Wooden batten 2 x 1in (5 x 2.5cm), as long as the finished shade is wide
> Lath $\frac{3}{4}$in (2cm) wide and 1in (2.5cm) shorter than width of finished shade
> Matching thread

Calculating the materials

Most upholstery fabrics can be used for Roman shades, as long as they drape well and do not crease too much. In most cases the shade will look much better if it is lined. The shade can be hung inside or outside the window frame.

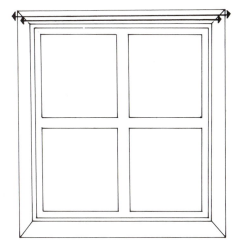

1 When measuring, use a wooden or metal yardstick for accuracy. For shades mounted inside the frame, measure the inside width as shown above and subtract 1in (2.5cm) from this measurement. For a shade mounted outside the frame, extend the shade width 3in (7.5cm) to allow for complete coverage.
2 When cutting out the fabric add 1$\frac{1}{4}$in (3cm) to the width for side hems and 6in (15cm) to the length for bottom casings. Cut the lining 2$\frac{1}{2}$in (6cm) narrower than the shade.

3 The shade is raised and lowered by a nylon cord threaded through rings attached to vertical lengths of a special tape for Roman shades, which are stitched to the back of the shade 10in (25cm) apart. The rings are spaced at regular intervals along the tape. You will need about two and a half times as much nylon cord as you need tape.

Making the shade

1 It is important to cut the fabric square, so tear across the fabric width to make sure edges are on the straight of grain.
2 Mark the center of each narrow side on both fabric and lining.

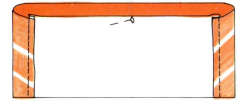

3 Place fabric and lining with right sides together. Pin centers together. Pin, baste and stitch side seams, taking $\frac{5}{8}$in (1.5cm) seam allowance. Turn right side out.
4 Match the centers again and press side seams, so seamlines will lie 1$\frac{1}{4}$in (3cm) in from long edges.
5 Pin top edges together.

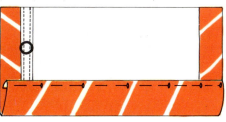

6 At the bottom edge, turn both fabrics up $\frac{3}{8}$in (1cm). Turn up a further 4in (10cm) and press. Pin hem in place.

7 Position and sew on tapes. Cut one piece of tape 3$\frac{1}{2}$in (9cm) shorter than the shade. Center this piece of tape over one side seam. Place top end of tape at top edge of blind and tuck $\frac{3}{8}$in (1cm) of bottom end of tape under hem edge. Baste in place.

Peter Pugh-Cook

8 Baste a second piece of tape over opposite seamline in the same way. Make

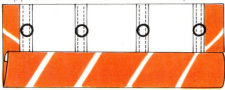

sure that the rings are lined up in a straight horizontal line; otherwise the shade will not pull up evenly.
9 Place two more pieces of tape, equally spaced between the first two about 10in (25cm) apart, again making

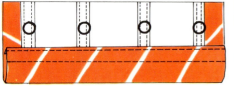

sure that the rings are lined up horizontally.
10 Stitch all four pieces of tape in place, sewing both sides of each tape

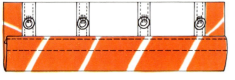

close to tape edges.
11 Stitch across hem, close to folded edge. To make casing for lath, stitch across shade again, 1in (2.5cm) down from first row of stitching.

Finishing the shade

1 Cut the wooden batten to the correct size. Paint it.

2 Mark and drill the fixing holes in the center of one side of the batten 2in (5cm) apart.
3 Check the shade length, allowing $\frac{3}{4}$in (2cm) for fixing the top to the batten and trim if necessary. Turn the top edges of fabric and lining inside to face each other. Pin, baste and sew together.

4 Tack the shade to one wide side of the

batten, the side which will face the ceiling. Place the tacks at $2\frac{1}{2}$in (6cm) intervals.

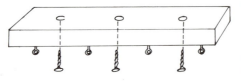

5 Attach the screw eyes behind the shade, along the front edge of the bottom of the batten, placing each one in line with a row of tape and rings.

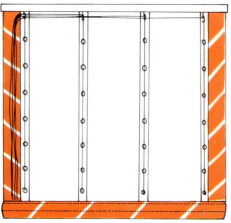

6 Tie one end of the nylon cord securely to the left-hand bottom ring. Thread the cord

through each ring on the left-hand tape, then through the row of screw eyes at the top. Let this cord hang loosely down the opposite side of the shade and cut it off even with the bottom of the shade.
7 Repeat step 6 to thread cord up through each row of rings.
8 Fix wooden batten in place in window.

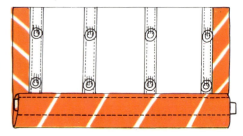

9 Measure the lath and cut it 1in (2.5cm) shorter than the bottom casing. Insert lath in casing. Slip stitch side edges together at hem and casing edge.
10 Check that when the shade is fully extended the cords are taut. Knot cords together at the ends.
11 Fix the cleat at the side of the window where the cords are hanging.
12 Pull up shade and wind cords around the cleat in a figure-eight. Keep shade pulled up for 24 hours so the pleats will form permanently.

Homemaker

Heather mixture

Use up all your fabric remnants in this braided rug. It is hard-wearing and perfect for brightening up a kitchen floor.

Finished size
The oval rug measures about 39 × 33in (100 × 85cm).

Materials
Remnants of tweed and other woolen fabrics—about 7⅝yd (7m) of 54in (140cm)-wide fabric
Waxed cotton thread
Tapestry needle

Preparing the strips

1 From all the fabrics cut out 3¼in (8cm)-wide strips. Cut each strip on the straight grain and make them as long as possible.

2 Fold each strip so that the raw edges meet in the middle of the wrong side of the fabric.

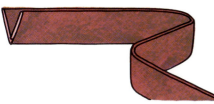

3 Bring the folded edges of the strip together to make a flat strip with all the raw edges enclosed.

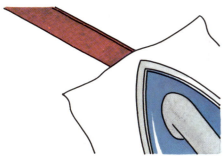

4 Press each strip with a hot iron under a damp cloth, or with a steam iron.
5 As you complete the strips, wind them around pieces of cardboard to keep them firmly folded, ready for braiding.

Braiding

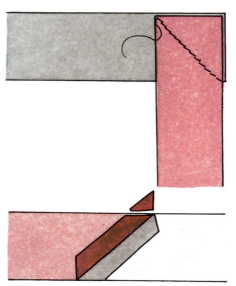

1 The rug is worked in a three-strand braid. To begin the braid, unfold the raw edges of two strips; pin, baste and stitch the two strips together. Stitch with right sides together and with a diagonal seam. Trim off the corner. Press seam open. Re-fold the strip, with the raw edges of the bias seam enclosed.

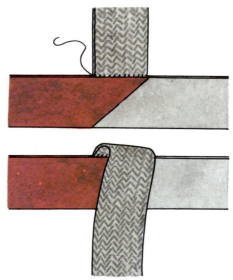

2 Position the third folded strip inside the first two strips at the seams, forming a "T" shape. Pin, baste and slip stitch the third strip firmly in place.

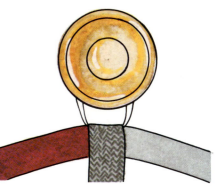

3 To work the braiding with the strips held taut, secure the "T" end either to a door handle or to a hook. This leaves both hands free for braiding.

4 Start braiding by bringing the left-hand strip over the center strip and then bringing the right-hand strip over that strip.
5 Continue braiding in this way, making sure that the folded edges of each strip are always toward the center of the braid. Keep the tension even, neither too tight nor too loose.

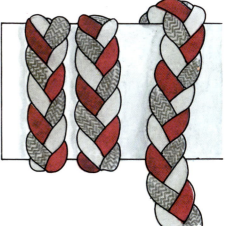

6 As the braid is formed, wind it around a piece of cardboard to keep it from tangling.

Terry Evans

7 As a strip ends, join on a new strip with a diagonal seam. It is an advantage if the strips are uneven in length, so that bulky seams do not all fall in the same place in the braid. Braid over a seam, so that it is hidden in the finished work. Braid a 7½yd (7m) length before beginning to sew the braids together in the oval shape.

Assembling

1 Lacing is the easiest and the strongest method of connecting the braids. Use a tapestry needle and strong cotton thread. Wax the cotton thread to make it stronger and keep it from knotting together while working.

2 To form the center of the oval, make the first braided length 12in (30cm) long before coiling. Then work around this central braided strip to form the complete rug.

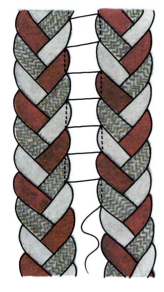

3 Lace the next row of braiding to the center strip. Cut a length of thread and draw it through a loop of the braid.

Knot the end and the working thread together to hold it, and slide the knot behind the loop.

4 Draw the working thread through the corresponding loop of the opposite braid. Continue diagonally up the braids, working through the corresponding loops of the braids.

5 Lace the braids together around the oval, keeping the braids flat. Do not lace them together too tightly or the rug will curl up.

6 Continue to braid strips and sew them together around the oval until the rug reaches the finished size. As the end is approaching, start to taper the width of the braids by trimming the strips to make them narrower so that they will gradually blend into the last round of the rug.

Terry Evans

7 Weave the remaining ends of the braid into the last round. Slip stitch the ends invisibly to secure them in place.

Spike Powell

Night and day

Two pretty, practical bags—a smart quilted bag which will hold everything you need during the day and a small clutch bag, ideal for a summer evening.

Tote bag

Finished size
14 × 8in (35 × 20cm). ⅝in (1.5cm) seam allowances included throughout.

Materials
½yd (.4m) of 36in (90cm)-wide quilted cotton print fabric
½yd (.4m) of 36in (90cm)-wide plain cotton and wool blend fabric
20in (50cm) square of cotton lawn
Two 6in (15cm)-long heavy-duty zippers
20in (50cm) square of polyester batting
Matching thread; tissue paper
1½yd (1.3m) of 3/16in (7mm) filler cord

1 From quilted fabric cut out one piece 15×9in (38×23cm) for base and two pieces 15×9⅝in (38×24.5cm) for sides.
2 From plain fabric cut out two pieces each 9×7in (23×18cm) for end pieces, two pieces each 25×3in (63×7.5cm) for handles and one piece 9×6in (23×15cm) for end pocket.
3 Using tissue paper and a sharp pencil, trace the pattern for the bag ends. Cut batting and cotton lawn into two pieces, each 9×7in (23×18cm).
4 Place one piece of the batting then one piece of the cotton lawn on the wrong side of one end piece. Pin and baste the three layers together.

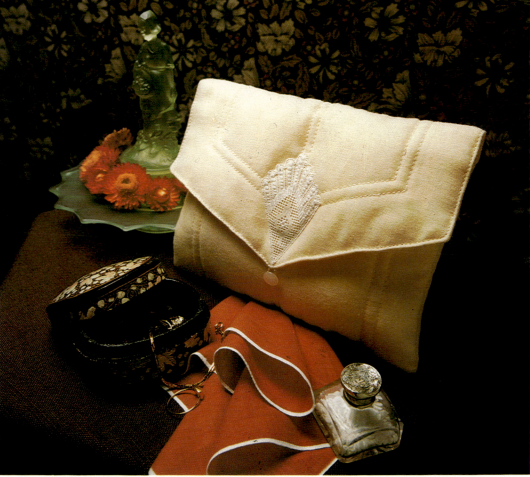

Geoffrey Frosh

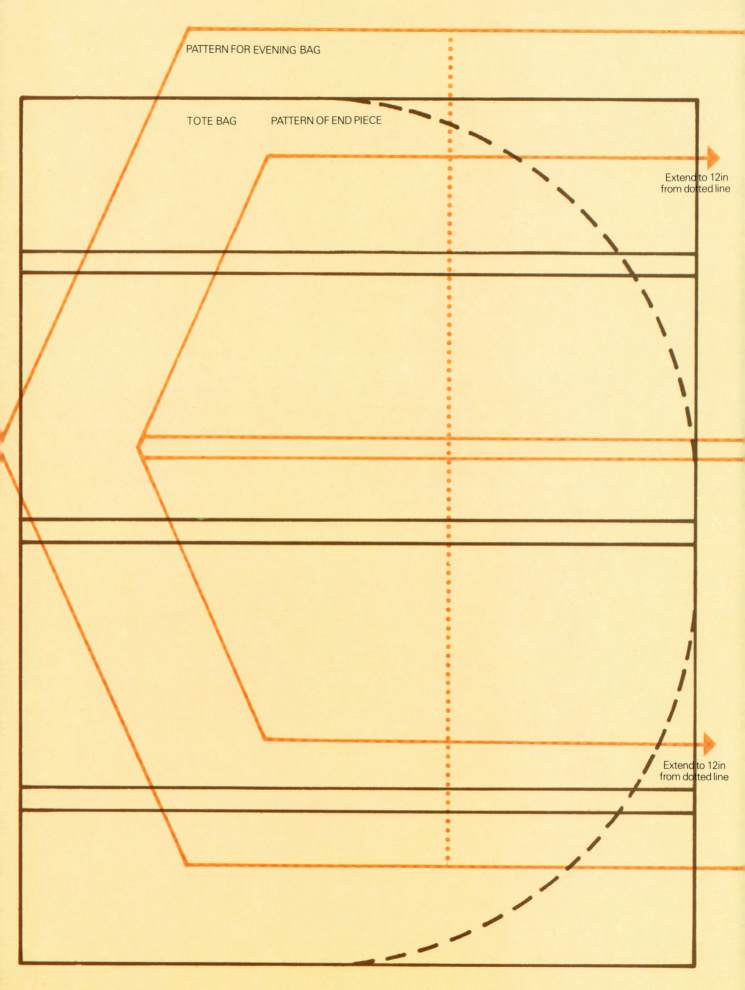

PATTERN FOR EVENING BAG

TOTE BAG   PATTERN OF END PIECE

Extend to 12in
from dotted line

Extend to 12in
from dotted line

PATTERN FOR EVENING BAG

126

5 Pin the tissue paper pattern to the right side of the padded end piece.

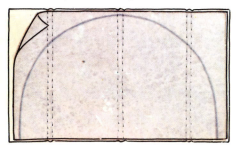

6 Work the double lines of stitching for the quilted effect following the marked lines.

7 Repeat steps 4 to 6 to quilt the second end piece.

8 Cut out the two end pieces following the tissue paper pattern.

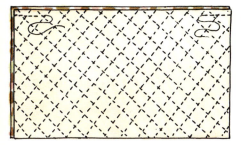

9 Place both side pieces together with right sides facing, matching all edges. Pin, baste and stitch along one long side, for 1½in (4cm) in from each short side, leaving the center open for zippers.

10 Fold the center seam allowances to the wrong side and secure in place with a line of topstitching along the length of the opening and along the seams at each end.

11 Pin, baste and stitch the zippers into the center opening, using the slot seam method (see Volume 4, page 68) with the zipper tops meeting in the center of the opening.

12 On one handle piece, fold under the seam allowance on the long edges and press them in place.

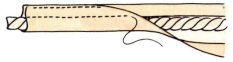

13 Cut the cord in half. Fold a handle piece around one length of cord,

matching long folded edges, so the cord lies in the center of the handle piece. Pin and baste in place. Stitch down the handle close to the cord, using a zipper foot. Stitch down the handle again, close to the folded edges.
Cut off excess cord.

14 Repeat steps 12 and 13 to make the second handle in the same way.

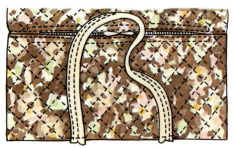

15 Position one handle on right side of one side piece, matching raw short edges to bottom edge of side piece, 3¾in (9.5cm) in from each outer edge and with cord lying toward the center. Pin and baste handle in place.
Stitch handle in place along previous stitching lines for 5in (13cm) up from base edge.

16 Repeat step 15 to stitch second handle in place on the opposite side of the bag.

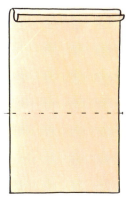

Terry Evans

17 On the end pocket, fold under ⅝in (1.5cm) of one short side and press. Fold a further 1¼in (3cm) on this edge to the right side and press. Mark 4in (10cm) down from this fold with pins. Fold up this section with right sides together, so that the fabric lies over the first fold.

18 Pin, baste and stitch side seams of pocket. Trim seams and cut diagonally across corners. Turn pocket right side out. Topstitch across the open edges to close them.

19 Center the pocket on one quilted end piece, 1¼in (3.5cm) up from base edge. Pin, baste and topstitch in place, strengthening the top corners with a triangle of stitching.

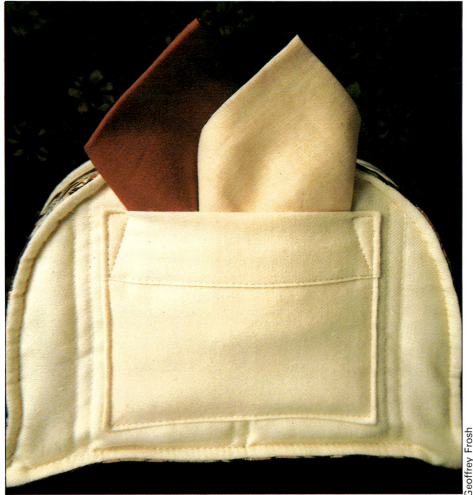

Geoffrey Frosh

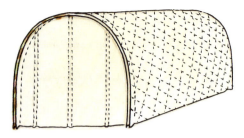

20 Place end pieces on short raw edges of bag side pieces with right sides together and edges matching. Pin, baste and stitch, starting and finishing $\frac{5}{8}$in (1.5cm) from base edges.

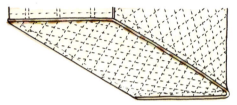

21 Open zippers. Position base against side and end pieces with right sides together and edges matching. Pin, baste and stitch base in place, starting and finishing $\frac{5}{8}$in (1.5cm) in from all edges, catching in handles on each side piece. Trim and finish seams. Turn right side out.
22 Topstitch seams about $\frac{1}{4}$in (5mm) from the edges.

Clutch bag

Finished size
8×6in (20×15cm).

Materials
$\frac{5}{8}$yd (.5m) of 36in (90cm)-wide cotton and wool blend fabric
One piece of polyester batting 20×12in (50×30cm)
One piece of plain cotton lawn 20×12in (50×30cm)
Small lace motif
One $\frac{3}{8}$in (1cm)-diameter button
Matching thread; tissue paper

1 Using tissue paper and a sharp pencil, trace the pattern for the bag, extending the six parallel lines from dotted line till they measure 12in (30cm) from it. Cut out the pattern.
2 From main fabric cut out two pieces, each $17\frac{1}{4}×9\frac{1}{2}$in (44×24cm). Cut batting and cotton lawn to measure $17\frac{1}{4}×9\frac{1}{2}$in (44×24cm).

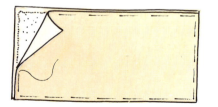

3 Place the batting, then the cotton lawn on the wrong side of one of the fabric

pieces. Pin and baste the three layers together.
4 Pin the tissue paper pattern to the right side of the padded fabric piece.

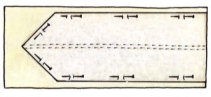

5 Stitch the two center lines of quilting following the marked lines.
6 Quilt the flap shape on the marked lines. Add a second line of stitching $\frac{1}{4}$in (6mm) inside the first line. Then, stitch along the outside lines.

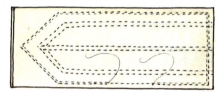

7 Place the quilted and unquilted fabric pieces together, right sides facing. Pin, baste and stitch the pieces together, following the outer line of stitching on the quilted piece and leaving a 4in (10cm) opening in one long side for turning.

8 Trim interfacing and cotton lawn close to stitching. Cut diagonally across corners. Turn bag right side out. Turn in opening edges. Slip stitch folded edges together to close them.
9 Baste around the outer edge. Topstitch around the outer edge of the fabric, close to the seamline.

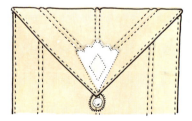

10 Measure 6in (15cm) from short straight edge and mark with pins. Fold up this 6in (15cm) section with wrong sides together to form bag. Slip stitch the two sides together.

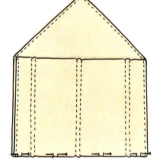

11 Position lace motif on center front of flap. Pin, baste and slip stitch it neatly in place.

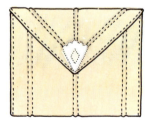

12 Fold down flap. Mark position of button on bag front. Sew button in place. Make a thread loop to fit button at pointed end of flap, working close blanket stitch over several threads.